The Transition to Stable Employment:
The Experience of U.S. Youth in Their Early Labor Market Career

Jacob Alex Klerman, Lynn A. Karoly

RAND, Santa Monica, CA

National Center for Research in Vocational Education
University of California, Berkeley
2150 Shattuck Avenue, Suite 1250
Berkeley, CA 94720-1674

Supported by
The Office of Vocational and Adult Education,
U.S. Department of Education

FUNDING INFORMATION

Project Title: National Center for Research in Vocational Education

Grant Number: V051A30004-95A/V051A30003-95A

Act Under Which   Carl D. Perkins Vocational Education Act
Funds Administered: P.L. 98-524

Source of Grant: Office of Vocational and Adult Education
                     U.S. Department of Education
                     Washington, D.C. 20202

Grantee: The Regents of the University of California
                     c/o National Center for Research in Vocational Education
                     2150 Shattuck Ave., Suite 1250
                     Berkeley, CA 94720-1674

Director: David Stern

Percent of Total
Grant Financed by
Federal Money: 100%

Dollar Amount
of Federal Funds
for Grant: $6,000,000

Disclaimer: This publication was prepared pursuant to a grant with the Office of
                     Vocational and Adult Education, U.S. Department of Education. Grantees
                     undertaking such projects under government sponsorship are encouraged
                     to express freely their judgment in professional and technical matters.
                     Point of view or opinions do not, therefore, necessarily represent official
                     U.S. Department of Education position or policy.

Discrimination: Title VI of the Civil Rights Act of 1964 states: "No person in the United
                     States shall, on the ground of race, color, or national origin, be excluded
                     from participation in, be denied the benefits of, or be subjected to
                     discrimination under any program or activity receiving federal financial
                     assistance." Title IX of the Education Amendments of 1972 states: "No
                     person in the United States shall, on the basis of sex, be excluded from
                     participation in, be denied the benefits of, or be subjected to discrimination
                     under any education program or activity receiving federal financial
                     assistance." Therefore, the National Center for Research in Vocational
                     Education project, like every program or activity receiving financial assis-
                     tance from the U.S. Department of Education, must be operated in com-
                     pliance with these laws.

Preface

This report uses data from the National Longitudinal Survey—Youth to examine the dynamics of the labor market experiences of young people entering the labor market. We confirm the conventional wisdom that young people hold a large number of jobs. However, our analysis shows that, by their early twenties, most young people have entered *stable employment*, defined as a job that will last one, two, or even three years. While there may be problems with the skills of labor market entrants, most young people are successfully finding jobs that yield long-term employment relations. The experience of the average youth, however, hides important subgroup differences. The results suggest that efforts to improve the school-to-work transition need to focus on those specific groups who fare worst in their early labor market career—most notably, high school dropouts.

The work reported here was jointly funded by the National Center for Research in Vocational Education, University of California, Berkeley, and the RAND Institute on Education and Training. It should be of interest to researchers and policymakers who are concerned with the early labor market experiences of youth in the United States. Selected results from this research have been published separately as "Young Men and the Transition to Stable Employment," in *The Monthly Labor Review*, Volume 117, Number 8, August 1994, pp. 31–48. The article is also available as RAND Reprint RP-338.

Contents

Figures

Tables

Summary

One frequently heard criticism of the U.S. educational system is that it fails to provide a smooth transition from school to work for those students who proceed directly from high school graduation to the labor market. Such young people are often characterized as facing a "floundering period"—from high school graduation through their mid-twenties—during which they move in and out of the labor force, holding numerous jobs, none for very long, and experience interspersed periods of non-employment. Instead of settling into longer-term jobs, these youth are portrayed as "milling about" or "churning"—i.e., not holding any job for very long and having no clear career progression (e.g., Osterman, 1980; Commission on the Skills of the American Workforce, 1990; Rosenbaum et al., 1990; Prewo, 1993; Osterman and Iannozzi, 1993). In contrast, foreign education systems are often characterized as involving a close relationship between schools and employers. Formal institutions, such as apprenticeships in Germany, and informal institutions, such as the "contracts" between Japanese schools and employers, help students in other countries gain the skills employers want, then help the students make smooth transitions from school to work (Hamilton, 1990; Rosenbaum and Kariya, 1989; Prewo, 1993).

In this report, we explore whether the above characterization of the transition from school to work is accurate for most U.S. youth. To do so, we use longitudinal data on a recent cohort of young adults from the National Longitudinal Survey—Youth (NLS-Y). We stratify by schooling attainment when the young adults first permanently leave school (which we call *school-leaving groups*) and compute static measures of labor market behavior—the percentage employed, in school, working part time, and neither working nor in school. We then turn to more dynamic measures—the number of jobs held and, our preferred measure, age at entrance into the first job that will last various lengths of time—specifically one, two, and three years. We view the time to reach tenure in a job of one, two, and three years as the period of "settling down" into *stable employment*, which is measured by job duration. Although we do not examine the characteristics of those jobs with extended tenure (e.g., wages or other aspects of job quality), we think our approach offers one useful way to begin to characterize the amount of milling about in the labor market by U.S. youth.

Findings

Consistent with the previous literature, we found that young U.S. men hold a large number of jobs in their first few years in the labor market (even after excluding jobs held in addition to full-time schooling). We also confirmed the results documented in previous research that a large share of young males are neither in school nor working full time after leaving school. This not-in-school/not-working status is especially prevalent among those who leave school prior to obtaining any post-secondary education.

Settling Down Occurs Earlier

Nonetheless, our analysis of age at entrance to a job lasting *M* years provides little support for the conventional wisdom that the typical male high school graduate does not settle into a long-term employment relationship until his mid-twenties. For the NLS-Y cohort, the median male high school graduate entered a job that would last more than one year shortly after his 19th birthday, a job that would last more than two years shortly after his 20th birthday, and a job that would last longer than three years while he was 22. If we exclude those who return to school—taking themselves out of the transition from school to work—the entrance into stable employment occurs even earlier, at ages 19, 20, and 21 for 1-, 2-, and 3-year jobs, respectively.

Diversity Is Exhibited Within and Across School-Leaving Groups

There is, however, considerable diversity within the school-leaving groups (SLGs) we examined. The above characterization holds for the male high school graduate at the middle (50th percentile) of the job-duration distribution. Thus, half of the men in this school-leaving group achieve stable employment at an even faster pace, while the other half proceed more slowly. For instance, male high school graduates at the 75th percentile of the job-tenure distribution do not reach a 1-, 2-, or 3-year-tenure job until the ages of 20, 23, and 25, whereas those at the 25th percentile attain these milestones two, five, and six years earlier, respectively.

There is also heterogeneity across school-leaving groups. While the median high school graduate entered his "three-year job" while he was 22, the median high school dropout, who first entered the labor force several years earlier, did not enter that job until he was 23. In contrast, the median college graduate—who entered the labor force four years later than the high school graduate—entered his "three-year job" shortly after turning 23.

Racial and Ethnic Groups Reveal Sharp Contrasts

There are sharp contrasts, as well, between black, Hispanic, and white men. At any point in time, black men are more likely to be neither in a job nor in school than are Hispanic or white men, and their rates of full-time employment are correspondingly lower. From a dynamic perspective, young black men in their early career hold fewer jobs compared with white men, and Hispanic men usually fall somewhere in between. Despite these differences, when we examine the transition to stable employment for the typical, or median, male with at least a high school degree, the patterns are remarkably similar across the three race/ethnic groups. However, at the lower tail of the distribution, black male high school graduates make the transition more slowly than whites, and minority high school dropouts lag behind their white counterparts in the transition to stable employment.

Women's Experience Differs from Men's

The early career transition for women differs, in turn, from that of men. While women hold fewer jobs on average compared with men at the same age, they do not always make a transition more rapidly into a job that will last one, two, or three years. This difference between the experiences of women and men is especially large for women high school dropouts and high school graduates.

Which Concept of Job Duration Is Used Makes a Difference

We further document that the proportion of young people who could be considered as "milling about" is sensitive to the concept of *job duration* used. Our concept—ever having entered a job that would last *M* years—presents a more favorable view of the transition than analyses based on whether the *current* job *will last M* years, or whether the *current* job *has already lasted M* years. And, we believe that our concept is the most natural one, because it is based on the experience of *ever* holding a job for a given tenure. We are inclined to believe that, compared with our concept, whether a current job has lasted or will last that long is of less importance: According to standard search models, some job turnover follows from the process of trying out different jobs, thereby producing better matches between an individual's skills and the needs of the employer.

Stability Through Time Differs for Some Groups

Most of the cohort of youth surveyed in the NLS-Y entered the labor market in the early 1980s. Considerable interest (and concern) has been expressed about whether, compared with earlier cohorts, this cohort has had a harder time making the transition from school to work. Similarly, there are concerns that the transition has become even more difficult, because the NLS-Y cohort entered the labor market in the early 1980s. To address this issue, we analyzed supplemental data from the Current Population Survey (CPS) to place the experiences of the NLS-Y youth cohort in the context of the experiences of earlier and later birth cohorts.

For young men with at least a high school degree, the picture that emerges is one of relatively stable early labor market experience during the last 25 years. The fraction of high school graduates, those with some college, and college graduates engaged in work or school between the ages of 19 and 29 changed little during the 1970s and 1980s. Likewise, job-tenure distributions for young men in the mid-1980s (the period covered by the NLS-Y data) look similar to those for the early 1970s and for the early 1990s. Thus, we conclude that our NLS-Y–based characterization of the transition to stable employment is likely to reflect the experiences of earlier and later cohorts of U.S. youth.

The lowest schooling group, high school dropouts, is the exception to this general picture of stability through time. Compared with earlier cohorts, young dropouts are increasingly less likely to be working full time and more likely to be neither working nor in school. At the same time, the job-tenure distribution for these less educated youth appears to have worsened through the 1970s and 1980s, with the largest effect being most apparent at older ages and longer-tenure points. These results imply that our NLS-Y–based characterization of the transition to stable employment for high school dropouts is probably too pessimistic for the early 1970s and too optimistic for the early 1990s.

Conclusions

The early career is a dynamic period, with transitions in and out of the labor force, and between jobs of various durations. The employment histories provided in the NLS-Y reveal that this period can be characterized as one in which numerous jobs are held but in which the time until one of these jobs lasts several years occurs relatively soon after leaving school. Our analysis relies upon a different and, we argue, preferable measure compared with previous studies. As a result, we find less support for the common perception that the typical high school graduate mills about in the labor market until well into his twenties. By our estimates, he will enter a long-term job (two or three years at least) in his early twenties—not the mid- or late twenties claimed by some other analysts. While the median high school graduate does not move immediately from school to a job lasting several years, making the transition to more stable employment does not appear to be a major problem. Such longer-tenure jobs may be "dead-end" by other criteria (absolute earnings, benefits, job satisfaction, earnings growth), but not by their longevity.

From a policy perspective, these results contradict the stylized facts underlying current school-to-work initiatives, many of which are predicated on the belief that the school-to-work transition involves periods of milling about that last into the mid-twenties. For most high school graduates, however, we found that stable employment (as defined in this analysis) is attained relatively quickly (by the early twenties). Thus, programs to encourage the transition to longer-tenure jobs may be based on erroneous perceptions of the school-to-work transition of most (but not all) high school graduates.

At the same time, our analysis indicates that youth who leave school before completing a high school degree may be the more appropriate target of such initiatives, because they take considerably more time to achieve longer tenure with a given employer. Finally, these results cast doubt on the suggestion that employers may be reluctant to provide training to young workers because they are concerned that young workers will leave before the firm recovers the cost of training. At least among high school graduates and those who enter the labor market with additional post-secondary schooling, there is evidence of stable employment early in the labor market career.

Acknowledgments

The research reported here was supported by the National Center for Research in Vocational Education at the University of California, Berkeley, and RAND's Institute on Education and Training. The report has benefited from the comments of Julian Betts, David Finegold, and Norton Grubb. Thomas Bailey, Robert Schoeni, and Kenneth Gray provided helpful reviews of the report. Sally Carson, Marian Oshiro, and Jan Hartman provided superb computer programming support, and Tanya Burton produced the numerous tables and graphs. We are grateful to Natasha Kostan and Courtland Reichman for help in preparing the manuscript.

1. Introduction

> Although the vast majority of our young people leave high school to go
> directly to work, we typically offer them little or no assistance in this
> transition. . . . The result is that typical high school graduates mill about in
> the labor market, moving from one dead-end job to another until the age of
> 23 or 24.
>
> —Commission on the Skills of the American Workforce, 1990, p. 46

In the debate about U.S. competitiveness, the U.S. educational system is
frequently accused of preparing students poorly for the school-to-work
transition. This poor preparation has two components: the content of the
education the students receive, and (given their skills) the assistance the
educational system provides to the students in finding jobs (Commission on the
Skills of the American Workforce [CSAW], 1990; Rosenbaum et al., 1990; General
Accounting Office, 1991; Prewo, 1993; Osterman and Iannozzi, 1993).

Non–college-bound youth in the United States are described as drifting from
activity to activity until their mid-twenties, when (it is hoped) they settle into
long-term commitments to full-time jobs. During the time between leaving
school and finding primary-sector jobs, young people are perceived as spending
a long period of unproductive time in school, in dead-end jobs, unemployed, or
not even looking for work, with a "consequent loss of training and productivity"
(Rosenbaum et al., 1990). For example, Osterman and Iannozzi (1993, p. 4) write
that

> [t]he early years in the labor market for many graduating students are
> characterized not by an absence of jobs but rather by a "churning" process.
> High turnover and frequent job change are evident during this period
> when youth sample different jobs or simply move from one low-skill job to
> another. The phenomenon of churning represents a characteristic of the
> youth labor market that has important implications for program design. . . .
> What happens when the period of churning has concluded? Evidence
> suggests that a substantial fraction of this cohort has been unable to "settle
> down" into quality jobs. In the past, most youth in their late twenties—
> even if they did not attend college—could expect eventually to obtain
> stable employment; this is no longer true . . . as many as 50 percent of high
> school youth had not found a steady job by the time they reached their late
> twenties.

This characterization implies that the transition period is spent unproductively.
An alternative perspective characterizes this period as productive "job shopping"

(Johnson, 1978; McCall, 1990): In the individual-choice-oriented U.S. society, young people try out various jobs until they find something amenable to their tastes and abilities (see also Meyer and Wise, 1982; Manski and Wise, 1983; Topel and Ward, 1992). Perhaps in other, less individual-oriented societies, the worker adjusts to the job rather than vice versa.

In this section, we draw on the human capital and job-matching literatures to provide theoretical perspectives for our empirical work on the early labor market career. We begin by considering the arguments that job turnover in the early career has negative consequences. The counter arguments that we summarize next view early career job turnover in a more positive light. We end this discussion by noting that differing values and underlying assumptions may play an important role in the divergence among the theoretical results of economists, assessments by policymakers, and the observed behavior of U.S. youth. A brief review of previous empirical research on the school-to-work transition concludes the section.

Negative Consequences of Early Career Job Turnover

The perspective that early career job turnover has negative consequences for youth is based on three concerns: those leaving jobs are at risk of being unemployed; those leaving jobs forfeit accumulated firm-specific human capital; and high turnover discourages firms from providing training. These concerns are discussed in turn.

The Risk of No Employment

Some of the concern about job turnover is prompted by the simple fact that, when jobs end, young people are at risk of being unemployed or out of the labor force. Such non-employment is intrinsically wasteful (disregarding the value of the leisure to the young person); potential output is sacrificed (Slichter, 1919, as quoted in Topel, 1991). Furthermore, inasmuch as workers build up skills on the job that can be used on other jobs (sometimes referred to as "general training"; Becker, 1964), no such skills are accumulated during subsequent periods spent looking for work or out of the labor force. Existing skills may even decay (i.e., be lost or forgotten) when youth are between jobs (Mincer and Polachek, 1974; Sandell and Shapiro, 1980). By itself, this argument implies that the crucial issue is not job continuity but being employed. This view is consistent with the general concerns in the literature about the fraction of youth at any given time who are unemployed or out of the labor force (Freeman and Wise, 1982; Rees, 1986).

The link between turnover and non-employment, however, may not be so strong. Based on a model of Burdett (1978), Parsons (1991) develops a model of on-the-job search behavior. In Parson's framework, it is often optimal to search for a new job without leaving the current job. Using the National Longitudinal Survey—Youth (NLS-Y) data for 1980 (which we also use below), Parsons (1991) found that half of all job quitters had already arranged their next job. Mattilla (1974) quoted similar statistics for the late 1960s.

The Loss of Firm-Specific Human Capital

A second concern about job turnover stems from the relationship between wages and time worked for a specific employer (often referred to as *job tenure*). If workers' wages rise *because* they stay longer on a particular job—perhaps because they accumulate human capital (e.g., they learn a firm's procedures or move up a job ladder) or perhaps because the firm can find a job that better uses the person's skills—then when the worker leaves the firm, he or she forfeits those higher wages and, assuming the higher wage was due to higher productivity, society loses output.

At face value, the empirical evidence is strongly supportive of the proposition that wages rise with tenure. Higher wages for more labor market experience, and an incremental premium for time with the current employer for workers with the same overall labor experience, are among the most robust findings in labor economics. However, there is controversy about whether the increased wages with greater tenure are evidence of a causal relationship (Abraham and Farber, 1987; Altonji and Shakoto, 1987; Topel, 1991). The alternative explanation is that the observed increase in earnings with tenure is merely a result of selection: If the people who left an employer had stayed, their wages would have been lower. Those who remain with an employer are increasingly a select group who are more productive with the given employer.

To consider the selection argument further, imagine a world with two types of workers: those who are highly productive and highly likely to stay with an employer (perhaps because they stayed in school longer and acquired more skills), and those who are less productive and less likely to stay on the job. If the more productive people earn more than the less productive people, and the more productive people stay two periods with an employer and the less productive people stay only one period, then the average earnings of all people in their first period of tenure with the firm is a weighted average of the wages of the high- and low-productivity people. Only the high-productivity people are left in the second period, so the wage in the second period of tenure is equal to the wage of the high-productivity people. Average wages of people with two periods of tenure are higher than those for people with one period of tenure. The rising wages with tenure are, however, not the result of tenure per se. If the job leavers had stayed, their wages would not have risen (see Topel, 1991, for more on this argument).

A job-matching story yields a similar type of selectivity. Suppose all workers are ex ante identical, but ex post some workers find that they can do a particular job better than others. Then at the end of the first period, people who find they cannot do the work well will leave to try a different job. Again, only the workers best suited for a particular job are left in the second period, and, by virtue of their higher productivity, they earn higher wages than those who leave the employer. Again, wages appear to rise with job tenure; and, again, if the job leavers had stayed, their wages would not have risen. Note that this second example does not require the assumption of the first—that more-productive workers are also more likely to stay longer (by their own choice).

Topel (1991) considers these selectivity arguments in detail and concludes that most of the returns to job tenure are causal. Despite these selection arguments, the longer a randomly chosen worker would stay on a job (on average), the higher would be his/her wages. This finding is consistent with declining turnover rates as workers gain job tenure. The more job tenure there is, the larger is the increment to firm-specific capital forfeited when workers leave a job.

Perhaps the most intuitively appealing evidence for this conclusion is the plant-closing literature. When a plant closes, workers lose their jobs through no fault of their own. If the selection model was correct, these displaced workers would be able to quickly find new jobs at approximately the same wage they earned on their previous job. In fact, even after controlling for the fact that plant closings tend to be serially and spatially correlated, it appears that displaced workers experience large wage losses, suggesting the importance of firm-specific capital or job matching (Topel, 1991; Carrington, 1993; Jacobson, LaLonde, and Sullivan, 1993).

If additional tenure generates positive wage gains, then when young people move from job to job, they forfeit their accumulated tenure (and its accumulated wage premium). This argument, however, is unconvincing in one respect: The young person leaving a job will bear the cost of the higher wages he/she forgoes from the loss of job tenure with the job change. If the worker is able to gauge the magnitude of those forgone earnings, he/she will leave a job only when the benefits of leaving (presumably an even higher wage on the next job) outweigh the costs (including forfeiting accumulated firm-specific capital). One possible explanation for early career mobility (which seems to have received little empirical study) is that job leavers are in jobs that do not provide significant opportunities for earnings growth with tenure. This is essentially the argument of dual labor market theorists (Doeringer and Piore, 1971).

Disincentives for Firms to Provide Training

The third concern about early job mobility is that the incentives for firms to invest in young workers may be weakened. In contrast to the preceding argument, which implies that skill accumulation (e.g., moving up the career ladder) is costless, other models suggest that workers and firms must jointly make costly investments in order to develop the skills that yield higher wages. For example, workers may be sent for formal schooling or paired with more experienced employees for informal training. In this context, job tenure is crucial. Like any investment, such training has a cost that the "investor" expects to recover in the future. Becker's (1964) theory of human capital divides such investments into two types: (1) *general human capital*, which will be productive (and thus yield higher wages) for other employers as well as for this employer, and (2) *specific human capital*, which will be productive only for this employer.

The work site may be the most efficient place to provide job training. That it is is a basic tenet of apprenticeships, co-ops, tech-prep, and other programs in vocational education (Berrryman and Bailey, 1992): By receiving training on the job, students see the relevance of their classroom studies for the world of work, increasing their interest and motivation. The use of academic skills in the work setting reinforces the skills learned.

To the extent that such programs provide only general training, however, firms have little incentive to provide it. The firm bears the costs of such training programs up front, whereas the payback to the firm comes later in the form of higher productivity. If the employer could reasonably expect the trained worker to stay with the firm (e.g., under a norm of lifetime employment), the firm could pay the worker less than the value of his/her output for a period of time after the training until the up-front costs of training are recovered (through the difference between the value of output produced by the worker and the reduced wage). But if there is high turnover, as soon as the worker receives the general training, he/she can command higher pay elsewhere and will leave for a higher-paying job with another employer or will demand higher wages on the current job. Thus, the firm would not recover the costs of the general training (Lynch, 1993).

Long apprenticeship programs provide one way around this problem. Young workers receive a low training wage even after they have received considerable training. The difference between the value of their output in the later part of the apprenticeship and their low training wage is used to pay back the firm for the cost of the training. However, in the absence of formal binding apprenticeships (or of the threat of withholding a certificate until completion of the full apprenticeship period), firms will not recover their investment and thus will not provide the training. Without such binding apprenticeships, everyone is worse off: The skill level of the workforce, the earnings of workers, and the economy's productivity suffer (Lynch, 1993).

The argument is more subtle in the case of firm-specific training. Again, employers have little incentive to provide specific human capital unless workers will stay with the firm long enough to recoup their investment (over a period in which the worker's wage will be lower than his/her marginal product). In the case of specific training, the value of the worker to other firms is no higher following the training investment, so the training itself does not give the worker an incentive to leave the firm. Nevertheless, early turnover will result in the loss of the firm's investment if the worker leaves.

With firm-specific training, only workers who are expected to stay on the job for a long enough time will be trained by employers. As long as young people are perceived (correctly or incorrectly) to have high turnover, they will not be provided with training. To some extent, firms can counteract the turnover problem by offering higher wages to workers with specific training. Since another employer will not benefit from the specific training and will only pay the untrained wage (assuming that the training is completely firm-specific and has no value to another firm), workers then have an incentive to stay with their current employer (Lynch, 1993).

Alternatively, a firm could adopt contracting solutions, requiring workers to pay, at the time of the training, for the firm-specific training they receive. The firm would then pay higher wages once they are trained. The initial payment for training could take the form of a payment from the worker to the employer at the start of the training; or in the early years of the job, the firm could pay lower wages than the worker could demand in a firm not offering training. However, the low productivity and small asset holdings of young workers make such contracting solutions difficult to implement. Low wages for younger workers mean that firms cannot lower wages much further because of the minimum wage. Small asset holdings mean that young workers have difficulty posting large bonds or funding the training themselves.

Compared with the two other negative consequences of turnover, this turnover-and-job-training relationship has consequences beyond the individual worker's own well-being. Although job leaving may be optimal from the individual worker's perspective, such turnover may create the perception that all youth have weak job attachment—a perception that will make firms less likely to provide training for young workers in the future. This potential externality (a cost imposed by this worker's actions on other workers) suggests a role for policies that provide new incentives or institutional mechanisms that overcome the barriers to investing in the skills of young workers and encourage young workers to stay longer with a given job (Lynch, 1993).

One attempt to encourage increased skills investment is proposals to formally certify job skills in particular areas. Job skill certification programs are motivated by the need for young workers to assure potential employers that they have acquired a necessary set of skills. Once a worker is certified, the worker will have a costless way to convince a new employer that he/she has the skills: Show the certificate. Thus, the training received becomes more "general" (rather than "specific"). Not only is the training inherently valuable to other employers, but now those employers can easily learn that a particular employee has the skills. By raising productivity both with the firm that provided the certification training and with other employers, the newly trained worker will be more likely to leave the current employer. This possibility will make employers less likely to offer the training, since they will not necessarily recover their training costs. Such certification might be good for other reasons—for example, it might encourage workers to get more training or make it easier for them to find appropriate jobs, thereby raising overall economic output—but it is likely to have the effect of reducing the amount of firm-provided training (Lynch, 1993).

This concern is consistent with the current institutional arrangement in the United States, whereby most training leading to a publicly recognized credential is paid for by the individual (e.g., at a technical school or other post-secondary institution). Firms are more likely to pay for training (on the job or otherwise) when that training does not lead to a credential. Formal apprenticeships, whereby workers pay for their training in the form of a training wage below the market wage (before they are certified), offer one way out of this dilemma. But such programs are rare in the United States.

Positive Aspects of Early Career Job Turnover

The labor economics literature contains several arguments that early career job turnover might be good. These arguments stem from a view of the early labor market career as an inherently dynamic process leading to an optimal match between the worker and a job.

A simple job-shopping model yields high levels of turnover at young ages, leading to a period of settling down as the worker ages (Burdett, 1978). In this model, workers begin their career qualified for a variety of jobs. Initially, they take the first job that becomes available but continue searching for a better job match. As new jobs open up, the worker compares subsequent job offers with the present job, taking the job offer when it is better (i.e., pays more) than the current job. As more job offers are received and some are accepted, the worker changes jobs at a decreasing rate, increasing his/her wage with each job change.

This simple job-matching model can be generalized to the case in which people as well as jobs vary (Jovanovic, 1979; Mincer and Jovanovic, 1981; Flinn, 1986). According to this formulation, different individuals have different productivities on the same job. While the worker may have some information about his/her productivity in a particular job, complete knowledge about the quality of the match between the worker and the job requires taking the job and gaining experience. This type of job shopping, then, involves taking a sequence of jobs; subsequent moves follow periods of learning about one's abilities. Job turnover leads to better and better job matches.

In addition to representing productive job shopping, employer changes may be an optimal career path. In the extreme case, if each firm had only a single job type, then, as workers matured and gained skills, they would have to change jobs to exploit their new skills. Obviously, firms offer more than one type of job, but it still follows that some career paths may require switching employers to attain the next job in the sequence (Sicherman and Galor, 1990).

The Role of Values and Assumptions

In our discussion of the potential negative and positive consequences of early job turnover, we have relied on two assumptions, both implicit in the current discussions of youth labor market experience. The first assumption, which is implicit in most discussions at the policy level, is that young people should either be working or in school; little value is placed on their leisure time. One interpretation of the observed high rates of non-employment among youth is that, in fact, young people place a high value on their leisure—it is worth more than the wages they are offered.

From this perspective, for example, the early work patterns of non–college-bound youth can be rationalized as an effort to equalize leisure with that of their counterparts in college (Nolfi et al., 1986; Mare and Winship, 1986). The college-bound peers of non–college-bound youth spend four years in an environment with a long summer vacation, several other vacations during the year, and a relatively flexible weekly schedule. The intermittent employment pattern of non–college-bound youth allows them to reproduce the leisure pattern of their peers at college. In general, if young adults value their leisure more than do policymakers, then two of the negative consequences of job turnover cited above (more non-employment and lower wages) carry less weight in terms of young adults' own assessment of their well-being.

In a similar vein, the second assumption, which is inherent in the labor economics literature (following standard economic assumptions), is that the young worker's objective is to maximize income (with some, albeit low, discounting of future earnings). If young people value leisure highly (or apply a higher discount rate on future earnings), then the assumptions implicit in standard labor economics models are incorrect. The valuation of leisure is particularly salient because several recent model-based analyses of youth labor markets were estimated only on the subsample of continuously employed young workers (e.g., Topel, 1991). By eliminating youth who make a transition out of the labor market, analysts may be missing much of the interesting and important variation in behavior. There is the potential for additional insight by reformulating the economic models of young workers' careers to explicitly account for the fact that a sizable subset of individuals may value leisure highly (at least relative to work). If so, the income-maximization assumption of such labor economic models is wrong and the interpretation based on them—that the transition is smooth—may need to be reexamined.

Previous Empirical Research

Despite the stylized facts cited in the passage at the beginning of this section and the various explanations of those stylized facts, the published literature on the transition from school to work provides contradictory characterizations of actual behavior. Rosenbaum et al. (1990, p. 264) represent the failure perspective. They begin their paper as follows:

> The transition from high school to work is a serious problem. Many high school graduates spend their first years after school unemployed or job hopping, with consequent loss of training and productivity.

Other analysts characterize the transition as proceeding smoothly (Meyer and Wise, 1982; Topel and Ward, 1992). For example, Manski and Wise (1983, p. 44), who analyze the employment experiences of male high school graduates, conclude that

> [t]hese graduates by and large seem to have made a rather smooth
> transition to the labor force and to subsequent schooling without
> substantial periods out of school and without work.

A more complex picture is provided by Osterman (1980, p. 16), who contrasts an initial moratorium, "a period in which adventure seeking, sex, and peer group activities are all more important than work," with a subsequent period of "settling down." His analysis of the NLS–Young Men and personal interviews suggests that the period of settling down begins for most youths within a few years of leaving school; some youths, however, fail to make the transition. More recently, Osterman and Iannozzi (1993, p. 6) explicitly link the empirical facts of churning or milling about to program design:

> For the bulk of youth not bound for college, the problem that public policy
> must address is not the simple absence of jobs but rather the difficulties
> these youth face in settling down into quality jobs in the adult labor
> market—a problem that has been exacerbated by rising skill requirements.
> If we accept a period of churning as part of the process, many of the ideas
> regarding improved information systems between schools and employers
> seem less compelling.

Before specifying policy approaches to address negative aspects of the early labor market career, we need to empirically examine the extent of milling about for the median youth and whether such churning is experienced by all youth. The empirical facts and their interpretation are relevant for policymakers and educators who seek to design programs to improve the transition from school to work. In the next subsection, we discuss our approach to addressing these empirical issues for a recent cohort of U.S. youth entering the labor market.

Plan of the Report

Our analysis of the early labor market transition for U.S. youth begins with a description of our main data source, the National Longitudinal Survey—Youth, and our methods. Section 3 presents the empirical results of the school-to-work transition in a static framework—labor force status at a given age; Section 4 presents results based on a dynamic perspective—number of jobs held and job duration. Section 5 uses time series of cross-sectional data from two supplements to the Current Population Survey (CPS) to put the narrow cohort data of the NLS-Y into historical context. The report concludes with a summary of the results, in Section 6.

2. The National Longitudinal Survey—Youth Data

Most of the empirical work that follows uses the National Longitudinal Survey—Youth. This Department of Labor–sponsored panel survey began with 12,781 young people (in the civilian sample) aged 14 to 21 in 1979 (Center for Human Resource Research, 1988). Blacks, Hispanics, and disadvantaged whites were oversampled. The sampled individuals were reinterviewed annually. This report includes data through 1990. Thus, this sample is now old enough (aged 25 to 32 in 1990) for us to examine nearly completed school-to-work transitions for a cohort of youth that entered the U.S. labor market in the 1980s.

For each year, the interview collected complete retrospective calendars of employment. Beginning in 1981, monthly schooling attendance records also were collected.[1] Using these data, we constructed monthly records of school attendance and work for each person in the sample for the period January 1, 1978, to the last completed interview date, usually mid-1990.

All the individual education and employment histories are censored (i.e., we do not know what happens at later ages), at least as of the 1990 interview, when the young people were aged 25 to 32. Furthermore, there is some sample attrition, so some of the data may be censored even earlier. To use all the collected data when computing time to events or percentage of people experiencing an event (by age or by time since an event), we computed monthly hazard rates.[2] We then transformed the hazard rates back into the percentage of people experiencing (or not experiencing) the event as of a given age or time since an earlier event (where the probability of the event not happening through age A is the product of the hazards of the event not happening at each age in months up to age A).[3]

---

[1]Prior to 1981, the NLS-Y data collected more limited information on school attendance. During that period, most (but far from all) of the sample were in school. Individuals who were in school and who appeared to be at grade level (given their age and previous answers to school enrollment questions) were assumed to have always been in school. Additional details of our procedure for filling in the missing monthly schooling information are available on request.

[2]A *hazard rate* defines, for all people whom we observed at age A and again at age $A + 1$ (where age is measured in months), the probability of a given event occurring (e.g., being in a job for M months) given that the event had not already occurred before age A.

[3]Although the raw data (on percentage of people experiencing an event) show some nonmonotonicity due to sampling error (and, perhaps, time nonstationarity, which is ignored in this report), this procedure forces the plots to be monotonic (i.e., the percentage of people who have received a high school diploma never drops).

12

Defining School-Leaving Groups

School-to-work transition patterns vary widely by schooling attainment when the individual leaves school. Not only does the age at school leaving vary with attained schooling, but (as we show below) the pace of settling into stable employment also varies. Following this empirical observation and the rest of the school-to-work transition literature, we stratified our analyses by schooling attainment at school leaving. However, the heterogeneity and complexity of transitions between school, work, and leisure make operationalizing the concept of school leaving difficult and make the results sensitive to the definition chosen.[4]

We assigned each sample member to a school-leaving group (SLG). Conceptually, a sample member has left school when his or her primary activity is no longer school. However, summer vacation should not be considered school leaving. In practice, we used the following algorithm. School is considered the primary activity for an individual only if he/she is attending school and is not working full time (FT; defined as 35 or more hours per week).[5] Given this definition of "full-time school attendance," we then filled in any gaps in school attendance that were probably due to school breaks (including the transition from high school to college). If the gap began in May, we filled in up to five months (i.e., May through September); if in June, we filled in four months. Gaps beginning in any other month were allowed to last up to three months without being considered "school leaving."

Once we determined that a gap in schooling constitutes school leaving, we set the date of school leaving at the first month of the gap and, for our analysis, assigned a permanent SLG to the sample member, based on school attendance and degree receipt through that date.[6] Even if the sample member later returned to school and/or attained a degree, the ascribed SLG is not changed.

Below we examine the importance of return to school and thus the difference between ascribed SLG and schooling attainment for an individual at a point in time. Given this algorithm for defining school leaving, we defined the hierarchy

---

[4]Other studies using the NLS-Y data define schooling groups according to schooling attainment at the end of the panel, which is not consistent with our perception of the way "high school dropout" or "high school graduate" is used colloquially or in the policy literature (see, for example, Veum and Weiss, 1993). In addition, such ex post classifications are difficult to use in our prospective hazard-based analysis strategy.

[5]We adopted this definition because the NLS-Y does not have a full-time school indicator. Before age 16, school attendance alone is used to define school leaving.

[6]People are not included in the calculations until they leave school and we can assign an SLG. This means that SLGs grow as people leave school (e.g., some of those in the "some college" SLG enter the sample at age 19, but many do not enter the sample until age 20 or later).

of five SLGs shown in Table 2.1, from the lowest SLG, high school dropout, to the highest SLG, those with some post-college education.

Sample Restrictions

Because the NLS-Y oversampled blacks, Hispanics, and poor whites, the results that follow are all weighted by the 1979 interview weight. That weight corrects for the oversampling and for differential nonresponse to the first interview. We made no further correction for subsequent interview nonresponse or permanent panel attrition.[7] All the results presented in this report stratify our samples by gender. The complexity introduced into female work histories by childbirth (whether as teenagers before they enter the labor market or as adults possibly interrupting careers) implies that the two-activity (school and work) analyses presented below fail to capture a crucial element of young women's work histories. For this reason, we looked at the patterns for women separately from those for men, and in less detail.

Since our analyses require complete work and schooling histories up to a given date, we imposed several important sample-selection restrictions. First, to ensure that we observed the beginning of the transition from school to work (and to avoid analyzing left-censored histories), we required that the individual still be in school as of the period covered (retrospectively) by the first interview (January 1, 1978). Thus, our high school graduate subsample should have graduated high school with the classes of 1978 through 1983. Our some college group and college graduates may include members of the high school classes of 1976

Table 2.1

Definition of School-Leaving Groups

School-Leaving Group (SLG)	Abbreviation
High school dropout	HSDO
High school graduate	HSG
Some post–high school education	SC
College graduate	CG
Some post-college education	BA+

NOTE: SLGs are mutually exclusive and exhaustive. An *SLG* is defined as schooling attainment when first left school for more than three months (up to five months over the summer).

---

[7]Our methods implicitly assume that panel attrition is random, conditional on the stratifying variables—gender, age, education, and, in some analyses, race. This assumption is consistent with most detailed studies of attrition bias (Klerman, 1992; Becketti, Gould, Lillard, and Welch, 1988).

through 1983. Finally, we included only high school dropouts from the classes of 1981 and later.

Second, we included an individual's experiences in the estimation only until he/she had missing data. Even if the respondent missed an interview but was interviewed at a subsequent interview, that information is included in our calculations only if we could fill in his/her experiences over the gap caused by the missing interview.

Combined with the sampling scheme for the NLS-Y (i.e., it is a stratified sample from several cohort-year groups), these sample-selection conditions make our sample extremely unbalanced. We oversampled men and women who were younger at the first interview and those who received more education. Table A.1 shows the weighted distribution of SLGs by age at the first interview, separately for men and women. For men, the percentage of high school dropouts decreases by 1.4 percentage points (from 35.32 to 33.95) between those aged 15 and those aged 16 at the first interview. The decrease is fully 9.3 percentage points between ages 16 and 17. The difference is primarily due to the increase in the fraction of men who left school before the retrospective period covered by the first interview, which began on January 1, 1978 (shown in the "<78" column of Table A.1). The proportion of men in this category increases steadily with the age of first interview, representing nearly 30 percent of the original NLS-Y sample. Similar patterns hold for women. Those individuals who were school leavers before the first interview are the main group excluded from our sample. Problems with missing data led us to delete another 7.2 percent of the original sample of men and 7.0 percent of the sample of women.

Table 2.2 contains the final sample sizes by SLG. The second column contains the raw sample sizes. For men and women, sample sizes for the first three school-leaving groups are well over 700, and for college graduates the numbers are over 300. The sample for the BA+ SLG is under 150 for both men and women—too small for analysis; consequently, we do not report results for them. The last three columns show the unweighted, weighted, and reweighted percentage distributions of the sample, respectively. The weighted column applies the 1979 NLS-Y interview weights. Those weights correct for nonresponse to the first interview. The final column presents our best estimate of the true distribution of membership in SLGs in the population. This reweighted distribution is computed by aggregating across the weighted distribution of those aged 14 and 15 at the first interview (from Table A.1). We use these reweighted weights for the analyses of the distribution of individuals across SLGs.

Table 2.2

Size of School-Leaving Groups for NLS-Y Men and Women

SLG	N	Percentage		
		Unweighted	Weighted	Reweighted
a. Men				
HSDO	1223	21.9	17.8	36.9
HSG	1235	22.1	22.3	35.3
SC	735	13.2	14.0	18.6
CG	312	5.6	7.4	6.7
BA+	119	2.1	2.7	2.6
<78	1498	26.9	28.7	—
Missing	457	8.2	7.2	—
Total	5579	100.0	100.0	100.0
b. Women				
HSDO	925	15.9	12.9	28.9
HSG	1308	22.5	22.5	39.6
SC	1005	17.3	17.6	20.9
CG	380	6.5	8.1	8.9
BA+	108	1.9	2.3	2.5
<78	1670	28.7	29.6	—
Missing	431	7.4	7.0	—
Total	5827	100.0	100.0	100.0

NOTES: <78   School leaving occurred before January 1978 (excluded from sample as missing data).

Missing   Specific data problems, in order of importance: unable to distinguish high school diploma from high school equivalency certificate (GED), left school during missing interview, still in school, invalid BA date (excluded from sample as missing data).

Reweighted   Weighted percentages within the observations for which we could assign an SLG among 14–15-year-olds at the first interview (among whom "<78" is very rare).

Percentages may not add up to 100.0 because of rounding.

Thus, according to our definition of school-leaving groups, in the early 1980s we estimate that the male youth population consisted of about one-third high school dropouts (36.9 percent) and another one-third high school graduates (35.3 percent). About one in five men proceeded directly to post-secondary education but did not receive a BA[8] before leaving school (18.6 percent); fewer than one in

---

[8]For simplicity, we use "BA" to denote all bachelor's degrees.

ten left school with a college degree (6.7 percent). Less than 3 percent proceeded directly to college and then directly from college to post-college education (2.6 percent). Compared with men, the fraction of women leaving school without a high school diploma is smaller (28.9 percent). The difference is accounted for by the larger percentage of women who leave school with either a high school degree (39.6 percent), some college education (20.0 percent), or a college degree (8.9 percent). A similar fraction of women leaves school with additional schooling beyond their college degree (2.5 percent). For both men and women, the high school dropout percentage reported here is considerably higher than that reported in most other sources, and the college graduate percentage is considerably lower (Frase, 1989; Haggstrom et al., 1991).

Before discussing our main results, we first reconcile the difference between the distribution of sample members by SLGs and the distribution by completed schooling. As we show below, this discrepancy is due to the classification as of when school leaving occurs and to subsequent return to school after school leaving.

Return to School After School Leaving

We assigned NLS-Y respondents to SLGs on the basis of their degree attainment as of the first time they were not in school (as their primary activity) for longer than the typical school break. Thus, by our definition, school leaving occurs when full-time work (with or without simultaneous school attendance) or an activity other than school attendance takes place for more than three to five months.

The assigned SLG does not, however, indicate the final degree attained. To the extent that individuals return to school, either by combining full-time or part-time work with schooling or by attending school only after a break in their education, the SLG and attained schooling will differ. Thus, for example, under our definition, some high school students may be working 35 or more hours per week and attending school. In that case, they would be classified as high school dropouts, even though they attain a high school degree in the usual time frame or some amount of post-secondary schooling.

Table 2.3 addresses the timing of school attendance and the extent of return to school, separately by gender and SLG.[9] This table presents the only results in

---

[9]The incidence of school return and final degree status are based on the information as of the last available interview, which varies across individuals because of attrition and varying age at initial interview.

Table 2.3

Percentage Distribution of Completed Schooling for NLS-Y Men and Women, by School-Leaving Group

SLG	Total		Returned to School (%)		Final High School (HS) Degree Status (%)			Final Post-HS Degree Status (%)	
	N	Percentage	Ever	Full time	Drop-out	GED	Diploma	BA	MA+
a. Men									
HSDO	1223	36.9	69.3	50.8	38.7	28.4	32.8	6.2	0.8
HSG	1235	35.4	61.3	31.0	0.0	0.0	100.0	7.9	0.6
SC	735	18.5	82.2	59.2	0.0	0.0	100.0	37.1	6.8
CG	312	6.6	59.7	22.4	0.0	0.0	100.0	100.0	13.5
BA+	119	2.6	55.9	32.2	0.0	0.0	100.0	100.0	54.5
Total	3624	100.0			14.3	10.5	75.2	21.1	4.1
b. Women									
HSDO	925	28.8	68.4	57.1	38.2	29.9	31.9	5.9	1.4
HSG	1308	39.5	52.3	31.6	0.0	0.0	100.0	5.6	0.9
SC	1005	20.1	78.0	57.1	0.0	0.0	100.0	31.0	3.6
CG	380	9.1	58.3	25.8	0.0	0.0	100.0	100.0	15.7
BA+	108	2.5	60.2	40.6	0.0	0.0	100.0	100.0	44.1
Total	3726	100.0			11.0	8.6	80.4	21.7	4.0

NOTES: The sample consists of all individuals for whom we could assign an SLG through the last interview they completed (through 1990). *Full-time school* is being in school and working less than 35 hours per week. Final degree attainment is based on the last available interview.

the report for "completed schooling." All other results are for school-leaving group, regardless of "completed schooling." In Table 2.3 we see a considerable amount of return to school, especially for those with incomplete degree attainment. For example, over 80 percent of men in the some college SLG (which includes men with associate's degrees) ever return to school; and about 60 percent return to school on a full-time basis. Almost 70 percent of male high school dropouts eventually return to school; over half return to school on a full-time schedule. Rates of return are almost as high, about 60 percent, for men who first leave school immediately after having completed high school or bachelor's degrees, although full-time attendance is much less likely for these groups. The patterns are broadly similar for women, although fewer women with a high school degree ever return to school. Compared with men, more women with post-college education are likely to return to school, and they are more likely to do so on a full-time basis.

While a large fraction of youth returns to school, completion rates are much lower. The figures for male high school dropouts help to explain why our dropout rates are higher than those reported elsewhere in the literature: Our definition corresponds to the general image of dropouts as those who leave school without attaining a regular high school diploma. Figure 2.1 plots the timing of school attendance and diploma receipt for male high school dropouts by years since school leaving. Figure 2.2 plots the same information for female high school dropouts. One-third of the young men in this cohort eventually received regular high school diplomas (i.e., excluding high school equivalency certificates [GEDs]), and nearly another third received GEDs. Not surprisingly, 95 percent of the high school diplomas (excluding the GEDs), and four out of five of the GEDs were obtained within the first three years of school leaving.

Thus, at school leaving (when the SLG is set), the high school dropout SLG represents about one-third of our male sample (36.9 percent). However, in the adult population—after accounting for additional schooling attained after school leaving—the high school dropout SLG is only two-thirds of that figure (24.8 percent): If we include GED recipients among the high school graduates rather than dropouts, the high school dropout group is only one-third the size of the dropout SLG.[10,11]

Across all SLGs, the pattern of return to school shown in Table 2.3 implies relatively standard schooling attainment rates. Eventually, 75.2 percent of the men and 80.4 percent of the women in this cohort received conventional high school degrees. Another 10.5 percent of men and 8.6 percent of women received GEDs. The remaining high school dropouts are only 14.3 percent of the population of men and 11.0 percent of the population of women. Another 21.1 percent of men eventually received college degrees, and 4.1 percent received at least a master's degree. A similar fraction of women achieved these two levels of higher education.

Thus, the distribution of the sample by SLGs differs from the distribution by completed schooling, because a substantial fraction of men and women reached their final degree status with gaps in their school attendance. Those leaving school without high school degrees are nearly evenly divided between those who eventually received high school diplomas, those who received GEDs, and those

---

[10]These high school completion rates for the population are computed by multiplying the share of individuals in the high school dropout SLG by the percentage of high school dropouts that ever gets a high school diploma or a GED. Since almost all such schooling attainment (through about age 31 at least) takes place within the first three years (see Figure 2.1), these numbers are a fair approximation for a recent cohort of the general population aged 21 and over.

[11]See Cameron and Heckman (1993), who argue that a GED recipient should be treated as a dropout, not as a high school graduate.

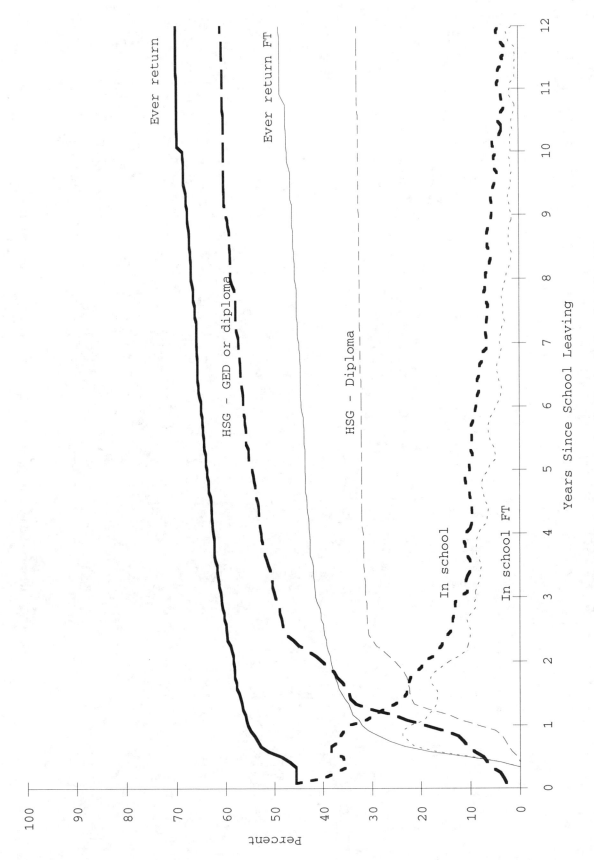

Figure 2.1—Return to School and Diploma Receipt for Male High School Dropouts

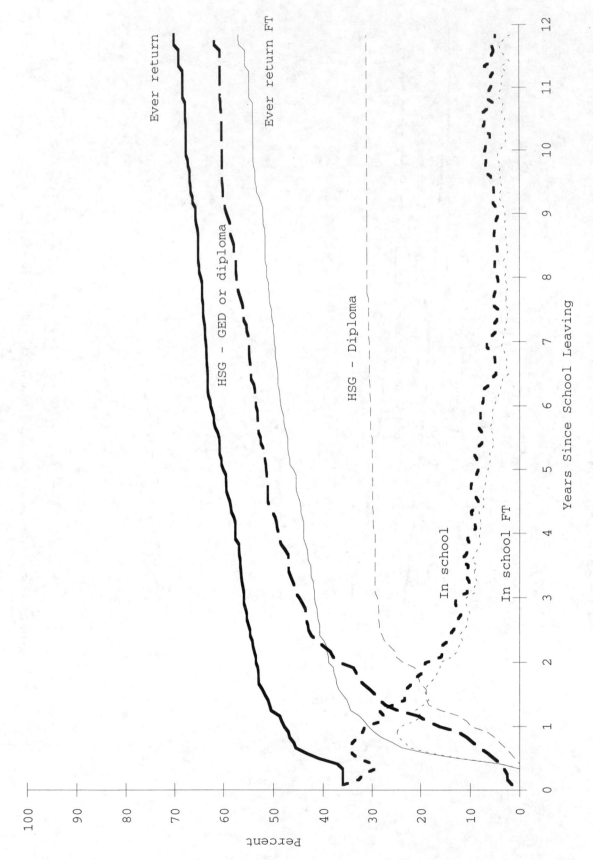

Figure 2.2—Return to School and Diploma Receipt for Female High School Dropouts

who received neither diplomas nor GEDs. Similar patterns exist at higher levels of education. Less than half of those who eventually received BAs remained in school continuously until they received their degrees.

Alternative Approaches to Defining School-Leaving Groups

As we noted above, operationalizing the concept of leaving school and entering the labor market is difficult, given the complexities of the school-to-work transition. We proceed in the body of this report to use the definition of SLGs outlined above, but we also examine the sensitivity of our findings to two variations. Specifically, above we define school leaving to have occurred when a young person works full-time (35 or more hours per week) for 4 to 6 consecutive months, even if he/she is also in school. Figures 2.1 and 2.2 suggest that this definition is problematic for high school dropouts: Nearly half of them are in school the month after we consider them school leavers, i.e., this is the first of 4 or more months (up to 6 months over the summer) of full-time work. Consistent with other analyses (e.g., Michael and Tuma, 1984), these results can be interpreted as showing that many high school students work enough to be classified as "full time."

To address the sensitivity of our results to this issue in the definition of school leaving, we replicate in Appendix B the set of results we present in this section and in Sections 3 and 4 for men, using a modified definition of SLGs that does not consider school leaving to have occurred until either the young person is not in school at all or has graduated from high school (at which time the 4 to 6 months of full-time work rule is applied). Using the modified definition causes a smaller (reweighted) fraction of the NLS-Y cohort to be assigned to the dropout category (29.0 percent versus 36.9 percent), and a higher fraction to the remaining SLGs, particularly high school graduates (39.4 percent versus 35.3 percent). With the exception of high school dropouts, the results are very similar to those presented in Sections 3 and 4 for each of the schooling groups. The alternative definition gives bleaker perspectives of the early labor market experience of high school dropouts than the results in the following sections.

Appendix C extends the sensitivity analysis by using the alternative SLG definition and stratifying the analysis by those who never returned to school versus those who ever returned to school. With the exception of those in the some college group, there is very little difference in the timing of the transition to stable employment. In general, those who eventually return to school take more time to attain longer-tenure jobs, as would be expected because they are more likely to have interrupted their labor market career. The magnitude of the differences by return-to-school status is modest, however.

3. A Static View of the School-to-Work Transition

Given our definition of school leaving (and realizing that there is some increase in schooling attainment from the initial SLG), in this section we present a conventional static picture of the employment activities of young men and women by SLG as they age. A similar, but not identical, description could be generated from a cross-sectional survey such as the Current Population Survey.[1] In the discussion that follows, we first analyze the patterns for young men in total, then disaggregated by race or ethnicity. We then examine those patterns for women.

We note at the outset that the static analysis presented in this section does not fully exploit the longitudinal nature of the NLS-Y data which allows us to measure time spent in various states as young adults progress through their early labor market careers. In the dynamic analysis that follows in Section 4, we use the NLS-Y longitudinal employment histories (for a given individual) to examine patterns of job holding and job duration over the early work career.

The School-to-Work Transition for Men

One picture of the school-to-work transition can be developed from the distribution of activity status of cohorts of young men at differing ages. Our analysis differentiates four activities defined hierarchically (i.e., those who might be included in more than one activity category are included in the earlier category):

1. Working full time (35 or more hours per week)

2. Attending school (and not working full time)

3. Working part time (and not attending school)

4. Neither working nor attending school.

With this classification, young men working 35 or more hours per week are classified as full-time workers even if they attend school. (This classification is

---

[1]It would not be identical because one cannot compute SLGs from the CPS. Instead, one would use current schooling. As we saw in the preceding section, the two concepts are not identical.

consistent with our definition of SLGs, but not with the alternative definition applied in Appendix B.) The activity status is determined as of the day the person turns the given age, rather than as an average over the entire year the person was a given age. An individual is only included in the sample once he/she leaves school and we can assign an SLG.[2]

Table 3.1 presents the distribution of the sample of young men at each age across these four activities for four of our five SLGs (excluding the BA+ group). The experiences of the high school dropout SLG are shown in panel a of Table 3.1. For this group, the data in the table are consistent with Osterman's (1980) view of "hanging out." At age 21, a quarter (26.7 percent) of males in the high school dropout group (31.9 percent according to the alternative SLG definition of Appendix B) are neither working full time nor in school, and through age 29 the figure barely drops below 20 percent (22.0 percent according to the alternative definition).

Panel b of Table 3.1 indicates there is some "hanging out" among high school graduates as well. Through age 21, more than 20 percent are neither in school nor working full time. As with the high school dropouts, this fraction comes down only slowly during the early twenties. Not until their 27th birthday does the percentage of high school graduates neither working full time nor in school drop below 10 percent (i.e., working part time or not working and not in school). However, the rate is still much lower than for high school dropouts at the same age, a group in which 19.3 percent is still neither working full time nor in school.

For the higher SLGs, it becomes relevant to ask whether we want to compare people by their chronological age or by their time since school leaving. While the rows in Table 3.1 define a specific age, each successive row represents approximately one additional year after school leaving. Comparing across the panels of Table 3.1, it is clear that the transition to full-time work becomes smoother as the amount of education acquired before school leaving increases. Beginning with the college graduate SLG, in approximately the second year after graduation (i.e., at the 23rd birthday), less than 8 percent is neither employed nor in school, and only an additional 6 percent is employed part time. The some college SLG fares only slightly worse. At age 20 (approximately the same point since school leaving), the fraction not working or in school is under 8 percent and their part-time employment rate is under 10 percent. The high school graduates

---

[2]As a result, the sample sizes increase in the early years, then decrease in later years because, by the 1990 interview, many of the sample members had not yet reached the older ages and because of panel attrition. Results are shown only if the cell size for a given age-SLG combination exceeds 150. When we disaggregate by race-ethnicity, the minimum cell size is lowered to 100.

Table 3.1

Static Labor Force Status for Men, by School-Leaving Group and Age

Age	N	Percentage			
		Working full time	In school, not working full time	Working part time, not in school	Not working, not in school
		a. High school dropouts			
17	437	51.7	16.7	9.4	22.2
18	820	48.0	20.6	10.0	21.3
19	1031	55.6	13.2	9.5	21.7
20	1070	62.7	9.1	7.0	21.3
21	1069	66.7	6.6	6.1	20.6
22	1056	70.6	5.7	6.4	17.3
23	1039	71.3	5.1	5.3	18.4
24	1014	73.1	3.3	7.0	16.6
25	992	77.9	2.2	5.8	14.2
26	898	77.5	1.7	5.3	15.5
27	661	79.6	1.1	4.9	14.4
28	412	75.2	3.0	3.3	18.6
29	193	79.9	1.1	2.6	16.4
		b. High school graduates			
18	446	58.4	4.5	19.8	17.3
19	1025	62.1	9.2	13.4	15.3
20	1173	66.6	9.4	12.3	11.6
21	1177	71.2	8.3	9.2	11.4
22	1165	76.5	6.5	6.8	10.1
23	1157	80.8	5.0	5.8	8.4
24	1143	84.2	2.4	5.9	7.5
25	1123	87.9	1.9	4.3	5.9
26	1035	87.4	1.5	4.4	6.6
27	817	88.9	2.1	5.2	3.8
28	598	90.3	1.0	3.2	5.4
29	376	89.3	3.6	2.1	5.0
30	183	89.5	1.9	3.9	4.8

Table 3.1—continued

Age	N	Percentage			
		Working full time	In school, not working full time	Working part time, not in school	Not working, not in school
			c. Some college		
19	165	66.6	10.3	13.4	9.7
20	385	64.6	18.6	9.4	7.4
21	536	63.6	23.6	4.4	8.3
22	620	62.0	25.2	7.7	5.2
23	656	66.0	17.4	8.8	7.7
24	675	76.4	10.6	5.6	7.3
25	668	80.7	8.3	6.9	4.1
26	634	82.9	7.2	5.4	4.5
27	516	85.3	4.9	5.1	4.8
28	425	89.7	3.2	4.2	2.9
29	323	87.0	3.4	4.0	5.5
30	228	85.8	4.8	3.1	6.3
31	156	85.8	5.1	2.7	6.3
			d. College graduates		
23	247	80.8	5.4	6.0	7.8
24	286	82.6	6.7	3.6	7.2
25	292	90.7	3.9	2.6	2.8
26	278	87.0	7.3	2.8	3.0
27	242	89.5	3.2	4.1	3.1
28	205	96.1	1.3	1.7	1.0
29	168	94.1	2.2	0.8	2.8

NOTES: N is the number of individuals in the sample at least through a given age. Results are shown when sample size for a given age-SLG combination exceeds 150.

fare much worse. At age 19, their nonactivity rate (neither in school nor working) is 15.3 percent and their part-time employment rate is 13.4 percent; and the high school dropout SLG is worse still at age 18, with a nonactivity rate of 21.3 percent and a part-time work rate of 10.0 percent. Thus, if we view full-time work as the normative state, the rates in the second year after school leaving for the four SLGs from the college graduates down to the high school dropouts are 80.8, 64.6, 62.1, and 48.0 percent.

As discussed earlier, an alternative perspective is possible. These high rates of non–full-time work are consistent with the leisure-equalization hypothesis discussed in Section 2. Figures 3.1 and 3.2 reinforce this alternative perspective. Figure 3.1 plots the fraction in each SLG neither working nor in school at each age, while Figure 3.2 plots the proportion in each SLG working part time at each

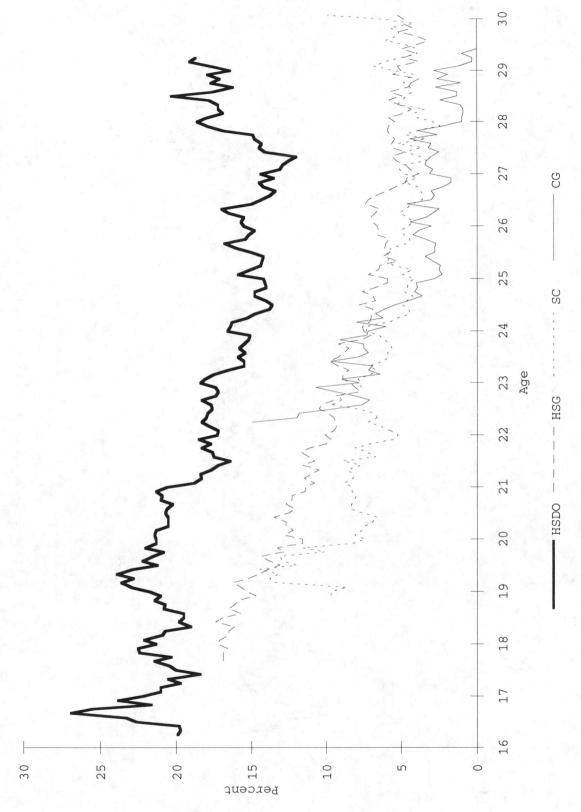

Figure 3.1—Percentage of Men in School-Leaving Group Neither Working Nor in School

28

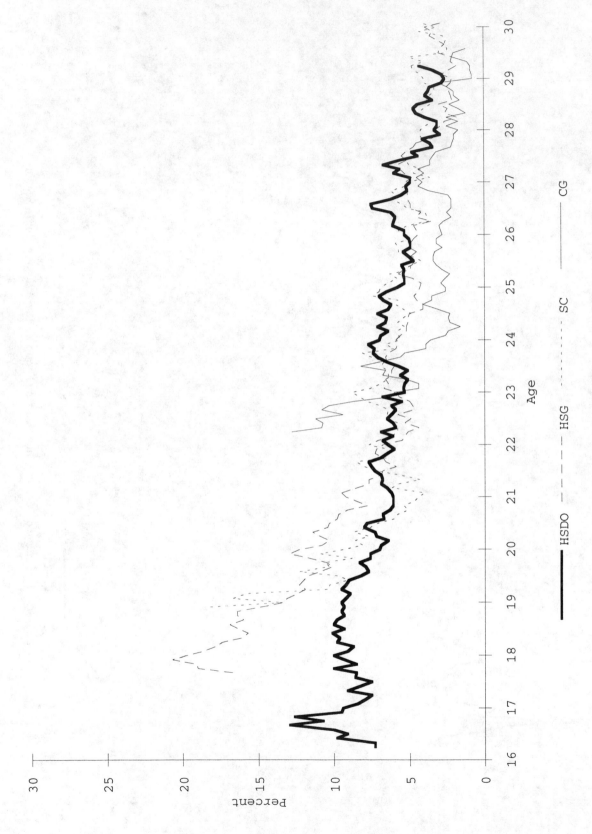

HSDO
HSG
SC
CG

Age

Figure 3.2—Percentage of Men in School-Leaving Group Working Part Time

age. Because higher SLGs leave school later, the line for each higher SLG starts farther to the right.

According to Figure 3.1, after age 25, once the nonactivity rate for college graduates drops sharply following their first two years out of school, the striking feature is the similarity of the nonactivity rate across all but the high school dropout group. The high school dropouts clearly stand out, with considerably higher rates of nonactivity over the entire period examined. The rates for the high school graduate and some college groups fall steadily as they age and their college-graduating peers leave school.

Figure 3.2 presents similar results for the fraction of each SLG working part time at each age. Again, except for high school dropouts, the other three SLGs start out with a considerable amount of part-time work. Such work is clearly transitional. Within a few years of school leaving (about three years for high school graduates, two for those with some college, and one for college graduates), the rates of part-time work fall sharply. Once again, however, the higher SLGs have a smoother transition, but the gaps among SLGs close considerably over time.

From this static analysis of activity status at each age, it appears that the outlier group is not the high school graduates but the high school dropouts. For dropouts even at age 23, the nonactivity rate is 18.4 percent, and their full-time employment rate is only 71.3 percent. At age 25, the nonactivity rate only drops to 14.2 percent, while the full-time employment rate attains only 77.9 percent— about 10 percentage points below the rates for the high school graduate and college graduate SLGs at the same age.[3]

Differences in the Patterns for Men, by Race and Ethnicity

While the figures for all men reveal that there is some heterogeneity in their work and schooling behaviors across SLGs, we can also examine whether there are differences in these patterns within SLGs by race and ethnicity. For this analysis, we define three groups of men in the NLS-Y: black non-Hispanics, Hispanics, and white non-Hispanics and others (primarily Asians). We refer to these groups as blacks, Hispanics, and whites, respectively. Although the NLS-Y oversampled minority men, there are sometimes too few black and Hispanic men in each age and SLG cell to make valid comparisons. For this reason, we are unable to make

---

[3]The comparison with the some college SLG is not appropriate, since many of them are back in school. Few of the high school dropouts are in school in their mid-twenties.

30

any comparisons across race/ethnicity groups within the college SLG, and for some of the younger and older ages in the other SLGs.

Table 3.2 shows the fraction of men at each age within the four activity categories by race/ethnicity, first for the dropout group, followed by high school graduates and those with some college. The basic pattern for the SLG as a whole is evident within the three race/ethnic groups. In particular, rates of full-time work are always lower for high school dropouts than for high school graduates, while the reverse is true for the rates of nonactivity. The differences between dropouts and graduates are of a similar magnitude for all three groups. For example, at age 26, 82 percent of black high school graduates are working full time, while only 69 percent of black dropouts fall into this category. The corresponding figures for Hispanics show a similar gap, from 82 percent to 72 percent. Likewise, among whites, 89 percent of graduates is in full-time work compared with 80 percent of dropouts.

Although the patterns are similar within the race/ethnic groups shown in Table 3.2, there are striking differences among the three groups in the distribution of men within each SLG across the four activities. The sharpest contrasts occur in the rates of nonactivity. At nearly every age, for example, black high school dropouts are more likely to be out of work and out of school than their Hispanic and white counterparts. Hispanics rank consistently in the middle, with the next highest level of nonactivity among the dropouts; the whites have the lowest fraction of dropouts out of work and out of school at any given age. For a given age, black dropouts are twice as likely as white dropouts to be nonactive. This same ranking (blacks being more nonactive than whites) is evident for male high school graduates, and the differences are again large. The pattern is repeated among those with some college for virtually all ages where a comparison can be made.

Differences exist within the SLGs, as well, in the fraction engaged in full-time work at any age. Here again, white men stand out as having consistently the highest fraction of dropouts classified as full-time workers. The pattern is broken only at younger ages for high school graduates and those with some college. While black dropouts and high school graduates typically have lower rates of full-time work compared with Hispanics, the two groups show very similar fractions in this status among those with some college. In fact, white dropouts look like black high school graduates in their rate of full-time work at each age.

The results in Table 3.2 are consistent with other data documenting significant differences in labor force participation rates and unemployment rates among white, black, and Hispanic men (Freeman and Wise, 1982; Wachter and Kim,

Table 3.2

Static Labor Force Status for Men, by School-Leaving Group, Race/Ethnicity, and Age

Age	N			Working full time			In school, not working full time			Working part time, not in school			Not working, not in school		
	B	H	W	B	H	W	B	H	W	B	H	W	B	H	W
a. High school dropouts															
18	201	177	442	43.3	47.5	49.0	15.6	11.0	22.8	7.0	16.9	9.8	34.2	24.5	18.5
19	293	226	512	41.6	53.5	59.2	10.4	8.2	14.6	12.8	9.5	8.7	35.1	28.7	17.6
20	311	232	527	52.7	61.3	65.3	4.7	7.6	10.3	10.1	6.7	6.2	32.5	24.4	18.2
21	315	230	524	57.1	62.0	69.7	3.6	4.7	7.6	10.3	5.2	5.2	28.9	28.1	17.6
22	312	229	515	60.7	62.0	74.3	4.1	4.0	6.3	7.5	10.3	5.6	27.7	23.7	13.9
23	307	223	509	59.2	69.1	74.6	2.0	3.7	6.1	8.4	3.7	4.7	30.4	23.5	14.7
24	298	216	500	60.6	77.5	75.6	0.6	1.1	4.2	8.0	3.2	7.3	30.9	18.2	12.9
25	294	210	488	63.2	72.8	82.1	0.7	0.6	2.8	6.2	8.1	5.4	29.9	18.4	9.7
26	263	194	441	68.7	71.9	80.3	0.8	1.4	2.0	6.1	10.5	4.4	24.4	16.2	13.3
27	207	133	321	68.9	75.8	82.9	0.0	0.6	1.5	2.8	5.9	5.3	28.3	17.7	10.3
28	145	—	179	68.1	—	77.1	1.4	—	3.6	2.2	—	3.7	28.2	—	15.6
b. High school graduates															
18	118	—	277	45.7	—	59.4	2.5	—	4.8	18.5	—	20.2	33.3	—	15.6
19	281	132	612	50.6	65.2	63.7	8.9	6.8	9.3	12.8	11.8	13.6	27.6	16.3	13.4
20	355	149	669	60.6	71.7	67.4	8.0	7.3	9.8	10.3	6.8	12.9	21.1	14.2	9.8
21	358	152	667	69.6	73.2	71.4	7.5	8.8	8.4	8.8	6.0	9.4	14.1	11.9	10.8
22	356	151	658	71.1	73.9	77.7	4.0	8.2	6.9	5.6	4.1	7.2	19.3	13.9	8.2
23	353	149	655	74.0	78.4	82.1	5.1	4.8	5.0	6.0	4.9	5.8	15.0	11.9	7.0
24	347	146	650	78.7	84.1	85.2	1.2	3.9	2.6	6.1	2.8	6.0	14.1	9.2	6.2
25	337	144	642	80.9	85.5	89.2	0.7	2.0	2.2	6.2	3.7	3.9	12.2	8.9	4.7
26	317	134	584	82.3	81.7	88.7	0.5	5.0	1.5	4.2	4.7	4.5	12.9	8.6	5.4
27	246	115	456	81.1	77.5	90.9	1.4	4.0	2.1	6.3	9.9	4.8	11.3	8.6	2.2
28	185	—	334	80.4	—	92.4	1.4	—	1.0	7.1	—	2.4	11.2	—	4.2
29	118	—	207	85.8	—	90.1	0.6	—	4.4	2.0	—	1.7	11.5	—	3.8

Table 3.2—continued

c. Some college

Age	N			Working full time			In school, not working full time			Working part time, not in school			Not working, not in school		
	B	H	W	B	H	W	B	H	W	B	H	W	B	H	W
20	100	—	214	51.9	—	67.1	23.4	—	18.2	11.0	—	9.0	13.7	—	5.6
21	138	—	307	52.5	—	64.4	24.1	—	24.6	7.3	—	4.0	16.2	—	7.0
22	167	103	350	59.5	63.0	62.3	17.1	11.7	27.5	9.9	12.9	7.0	13.6	12.4	3.2
23	178	107	371	65.7	65.5	66.1	12.6	16.1	18.3	10.0	8.9	8.6	11.8	9.5	6.9
24	185	111	379	74.5	72.5	77.0	8.9	13.9	10.7	9.0	5.2	5.1	7.6	8.4	7.2
25	181	107	380	77.1	74.8	81.7	6.2	15.4	8.2	7.3	3.2	7.1	9.5	6.6	3.1
26	169	101	364	77.1	75.4	84.4	3.5	8.6	7.7	6.1	7.1	5.1	13.2	8.9	2.8
27	137	—	298	77.8	—	86.5	6.1	—	4.7	5.9	—	5.1	10.2	—	3.8
28	111	—	246	85.9	—	90.2	4.4	—	3.0	4.0	—	4.2	5.7	—	2.6

NOTES: B = black non-Hispanic, H = Hispanic, W = white non-Hispanic and other.
N is the number of individuals in the sample at least through a given age. Results are shown when sample size for a given age-SLG-race/ethnic group combination exceeds 100.

1982). These differences persist for the three school-leaving groups we consider in Table 3.2. Thus, the patterns evident in the aggregate are not simply the result of differences in the educational composition of men in the three race/ethnic groups, but are due as well to underlying differences in early employment experience within different schooling groups. In Section 4, we further explore whether these differences are evident when we view the early labor market period from a dynamic perspective.

The School-to-Work Transition for Women

As we noted in Section 2, we stratified our analysis by gender because we expected that fertility among young women will differentially affect their schooling and early labor force patterns. While we expect more women to be out of the labor force or school as a result of pregnancy and childrearing responsibilities, we do not explicitly attempt to account for this "activity" in either the static analysis presented here or the dynamic analyses that follow in the next section. Here we present a set of tabulations that, while more limited, parallel those just presented for men.

We begin by calculating the fraction of women in each of the four activity statuses at each age, stratified by SLG. Table 3.3 reports results comparable to those we reported for men in Table 3.1. Figures 3.3 and 3.4 (comparable to Figures 3.1 and 3.2 for men) show the fraction of women neither working nor in school and the fraction working part time.

A comparison of the results for women with those seen earlier for men reveals the expected differences. The fraction of women neither working nor in school is higher at every age compared with that of men for the four SLGs shown in Figure 3.3. Instead of the decline with age in rates of nonactivity seen for men, the lines are approximately flat for women in the three lowest SLGs. Among women in the college graduate SLG, there is evidence of a U-shaped pattern: The percentage neither working nor in school declines until about age 24, and the fraction increases thereafter. This pattern is most likely the result of the childbearing that was delayed for these women until they had completed schooling and had begun their work career. Among women, there is less evidence of a convergence in the pattern across the three highest SLGs. The ordering of activity rates of the SLGs and approximate gaps between the rates for SLGs—more educated women have lower nonactivity rates—does not diminish appreciably as the women age. However, women with a college degree and

34

Table 3.3
Static Labor Force Status for Women, by School-Leaving Group and Age

Age	N	Working full time	In school, not working full time	Working part time, not in school	Not working, not in school
			Percentage		
a. High school dropouts					
17	348	32.8	23.3	13.4	30.6
18	636	33.0	19.4	12.2	35.4
19	745	31.8	13.1	14.8	40.3
20	778	36.6	9.5	15.3	38.6
21	780	39.7	7.8	13.6	38.9
22	775	42.2	6.4	11.0	40.4
23	769	44.8	5.4	11.3	38.5
24	760	47.3	2.8	13.1	36.7
25	745	49.8	3.1	11.7	35.4
26	697	49.5	3.5	13.2	33.8
27	499	49.8	4.3	12.8	33.1
28	302	48.4	3.0	11.3	37.3
b. High school graduates					
18	572	46.6	3.7	24.4	25.3
19	1163	47.5	8.2	20.3	24.0
20	1268	54.7	8.1	13.8	23.4
21	1265	54.8	7.6	14.3	23.2
22	1251	53.9	7.1	15.4	23.6
23	1233	56.8	4.0	15.6	23.6
24	1218	58.6	3.6	13.8	24.0
25	1196	59.7	2.7	14.7	22.9
26	1120	59.6	2.2	15.2	23.0
27	876	58.8	2.6	15.9	22.7
28	613	55.4	2.8	16.8	25.0
29	366	53.3	3.0	17.1	26.6
30	171	56.0	0.5	14.9	28.5

Table 3.3—continued

Age	N	Percentage			
		Working full time	In school, not working full time	Working part time, not in school	Not working, not in school
		c. Some college			
19	259	55.5	6.6	19.4	18.5
20	535	51.8	17.4	15.9	14.9
21	751	56.9	17.4	11.3	14.3
22	888	58.5	16.0	12.7	12.8
23	934	62.2	11.5	12.0	14.3
24	948	66.1	9.1	10.5	14.3
25	936	68.9	6.0	13.3	11.8
26	899	66.7	5.8	12.3	15.2
27	781	64.9	5.6	12.2	17.3
28	659	62.1	4.0	17.2	16.7
29	529	62.5	3.1	16.1	18.4
30	365	59.7	3.4	15.7	21.2
31	222	56.9	3.0	18.2	22.0
		d. College graduates			
22	183	65.7	2.0	19.9	12.3
23	336	77.0	3.2	10.2	9.6
24	360	79.2	4.1	10.2	6.5
25	356	80.1	5.3	7.5	7.1
26	348	75.0	6.1	9.5	9.4
27	309	73.2	6.5	10.6	9.6
28	272	68.9	6.1	13.3	11.7
29	235	65.7	5.1	14.8	14.4
30	183	64.4	4.2	11.8	19.6

NOTES: N is the number of individuals in the sample at least through a given age. Results are shown when sample size for a given age-SLG combination exceeds 150.

those with some college look more similar compared with high school graduate women. As before, the high school dropout women offer the sharpest contrast.

The pattern of part-time work among women, as shown in Figure 3.4, is also substantially different from that seen for men. At virtually every age, women in each SLG are more likely than men to be working part time. As with their male counterparts, there are few differences past the early twenties for women in the four SLGs; the fraction of college graduate women working part time is within a few percentage points of the share for high school dropouts. At variance from the men, however, is the little change in the fraction working part time as the women age. From age 20 to 30, roughly 15 percent of women are in this category.

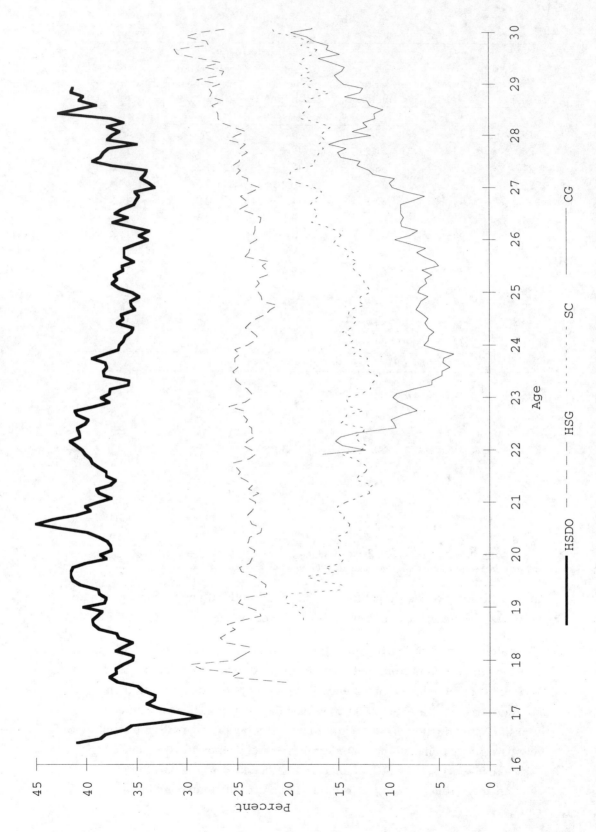

Figure 3.3—Percentage of Women in School-Leaving Group Neither Working Nor in School

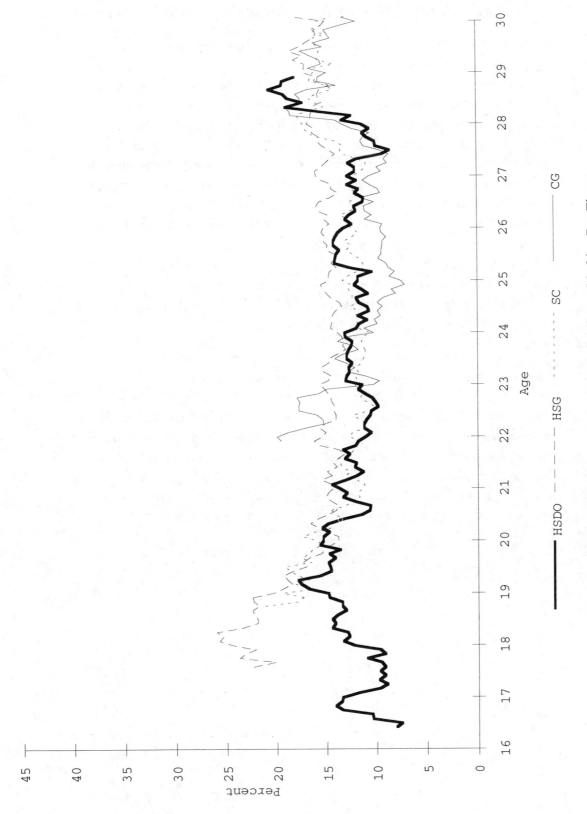

Figure 3.4—Percentage of Women in School-Leaving Group Working Part Time

The Static Perspective of the School-to-Work Transition

In this section we have viewed the school-to-work transition as a series of snapshots taken at each age in the early labor market careers of young men and women in the NLS-Y. When these series of snapshots are pieced together, we are left with a picture of the early labor market experiences that is extremely varied. For some—particularly men who leave school without a high school diploma and minority men in the high school graduate SLG—we see a substantial fraction who are not in a job and not in school. While fewer men are in this position by their late twenties compared with their early twenties, the fraction is still high even after more than 10 years of potential labor market experience. This fraction exceeds that experienced by men with more schooling, such as college graduate men, who appear to reach a high rate of full-time employment soon after leaving school. As we might expect, the patterns for women vary substantially from those of their male counterparts, presumably because women are more likely to take time out from schooling and work for childbearing and childrearing, responsibilities that may conflict with schooling and work.

While this static view of the school-to-work transitions reveals some important contrasts among young adults based on gender, school-leaving group, and race/ethnicity, the analysis obscures the underlying dynamics of the early labor market career. Should we take the static view presented in this section as evidence of considerable "churning" and "milling about"? As young adults move between the various states of work and school, how many jobs do they hold and for how long? Is the process of settling down similar regardless of schooling attainment at the time of labor market entry or other demographic characteristics? These are the issues we address in the next section.

4. A Dynamic View of the School-to-Work Transition

The perception that non–college-bound youth mill about in the labor market in the early years after leaving school is a statement about the *dynamics* of employment. The *early career* is characterized as a period when youth hold numerous jobs, many for short periods of time. Thus, we need to be able to measure the number of jobs held in the early career and account for the time spent in any given job. These inherently dynamic measurements are not captured in the snapshot view of activity status of Section 3, which considers only the fraction working or in school at any point in time. A major advantage of the NLS-Y data is that they enable us to go beyond such a static view to consider the school-to-work transition in this dynamic framework.

In this section, we use the information in the NLS-Y employment histories to further evaluate the employment experiences of young men and women in their early labor market career. We first examine the transition process in terms of the distribution of the number of jobs held at successive ages. We then consider the transition to *stable employment*, which is measured by job duration. We continue to analyze each SLG separately, first examining the patterns for men and then examining the patterns for women.

Number of Jobs Held in the Early Career

Several recent studies demonstrate that young adults hold a surprisingly large number of jobs early in their labor market career (Bureau of Labor Statistics [BLS], 1992, 1993; Topel and Ward, 1992; Veum and Weiss, 1993). For example, tabulations from the NLS-Y by the Bureau of Labor Statistics reveal that young men hold an average of 7.6 jobs between their 18th and 30th birthdays; the count is only slightly lower (7.3 jobs) for women (BLS, 1993). In this subsection, we examine this issue by considering the mean number of jobs held by youth at each age, separately for the four SLGs. Since the mean obscures the spread in the distribution of jobs held across youth, we also report the number of jobs held by the median youth, as well as by the young person at the 25th and 75th percentiles of the jobs-held distribution. Thus, we can assess the experience of the "typical" youth, and how different his or her experience is compared with a counterpart who is at the bottom or top of the jobs-held distribution. In our analysis, *jobs* are counted only after school leaving and are defined as employment with a given employer.[1]

Patterns for Men

For each SLG and age, Table 4.1 presents the mean number of jobs held by young men, as well as the number of jobs held at the 25th, 50th, and 75th percentiles of the distribution of the number of jobs held. Table 4.1 confirms that young men hold a large number of jobs in the years immediately after leaving school, a result that is consistent with the findings reported elsewhere (BLS, 1992; Topel and Ward, 1992; Veum and Weiss, 1993). For example, by age 28, high school dropouts have held an average of 8.6 jobs since they left school. The average number of jobs held at the same age declines for each successive SLG, with college graduates having held 3.6 jobs by age 28.

There are sharp differences by SLG in the number of jobs held during the early career.[2] Most notably, the number of jobs held by high school dropouts is larger than for the other SLGs. The median male in this group has held six jobs by age 24 and eight jobs by age 28. A high school dropout at the 75th percentile of the jobs-held distribution, in contrast, has held nine jobs by age 24 and more than ten jobs by age 28. As a summary measure, these figures represent about one job every other year at the median and one job per year at the 75th percentile.

The high school graduate group starts working about one year later (on average) and holds fewer jobs. After a year, it is accumulating about half a job per year at the median, less than one-third of a job per year at the 25th percentile, and about one job per year at the 75th percentile. Similar patterns exist for the some college group. Finally, the college graduates start about four years later than the high school graduates, and they accumulate new jobs the most slowly. Exact comparisons are difficult because most of them were still in their second or third job by the end of the survey.

---

[1]Our results will be different from those of other recent studies, which measure all jobs held starting at a certain age whether or not the youth had left school, and classify youth by schooling attainment as of the most recent interview date (rather than at school leaving).

[2]Our estimates of the mean number of jobs held for higher SLGs are lower than the estimates provided by other analyses. The reason appears to be that other authors (e.g., BLS, 1992, 1993; Veum and Weiss, 1993) count all jobs since age 18, whereas we count only jobs since school leaving. For this reason, we show fewer jobs at any given age for higher SLGs, while other authors (e.g., BLS, 1992, 1993; Veum and Weiss, 1993) find the reverse relationship.

Table 4.1

Number of Jobs Held by Men, by School-Leaving Group and Age, at Mean, and at 25th, 50th, and 75th Percentiles of Distribution

Age	N				HSDO				HSG				SC				CG			
	HSDO	HSG	SC	CG	Mean	25th	50th	75th	Mean	25th	50th	75th	Mean	25th	50th	75th	Mean	25th	50th	75th
17	1122	1225	729	307	0.5	0	0	1	0.0	0	0	0	0.0	0	0	0	0.0	0	0	0
18	1106	1217	727	307	1.4	0	1	2	0.4	0	0	1	0.0	0	0	0	0.0	0	0	0
19	1093	1202	724	306	2.5	1	2	4	1.5	1	1	2	0.3	0	0	0	0.0	0	0	0
20	1082	1193	721	304	3.5	2	3	5	2.5	1	2	3	1.0	0	1	2	0.0	0	0	0
21	1074	1179	707	303	4.3	2	4	6	3.3	2	3	4	1.8	0	2	3	0.0	0	0	0
22	1059	1168	700	301	5.2	3	5	7	4.0	2	4	5	2.7	1	2	4	0.4	0	0	1
23	1040	1160	693	297	5.9	3	5	8	4.7	2	4	6	3.6	2	3	5	1.3	1	1	2
24	1017	1143	687	295	6.7	4	6	9	5.3	3	5	7	4.4	2	4	6	2.0	1	2	3
25	994	1125	672	294	7.3	4	7	10	5.9	3	5	8	5.0	3	5	7	2.5	1	2	3
26	902	1035	637	279	8.0	5	7	10	6.3	3	6	9	5.6	3	5	8	2.9	1	2	4
27	662	817	517	242	8.6	5	8	10	6.7	4	6	9	6.2	3	5	8	3.3	2	3	4
28	413	598	425	2C5	8.6	5	8	10	7.2	4	6	10	6.7	4	6	9	3.6	2	3	5
29	194	376	323	169	8.8	6	9	10	7.6	4	7	10	7.0	4	6	9	3.8	2	3	5
30	—	183	228	—	—	—	—	—	7.8	4	7	10	7.3	4	7	10	—	—	—	—
31	—	—	156	—	—	—	—	—	—	—	—	—	7.7	4	7	10	—	—	—	—

NOTES: A value of 10 indicates 10 or more jobs.
N is the number of individuals in the sample at least through a given age. Results are shown when sample size for a given age-SLG combination exceeds 150.

Differences by Race/Ethnicity

Table 4.2 repeats the data on number of jobs held just illustrated for all men, separately by the three race/ethnic groups considered previously. Within the three groups of men, it is still the case that both the mean and median number of jobs held is higher at each age for lower SLGs. At the same time, for Hispanic and white males the contrast between high school dropouts and high school graduates is sharper than it is for black males. For example, at age 26, the average black male high school dropout has held about three-fourths of a job more than the average high school graduate, whereas the average white or Hispanic dropout has held almost 2 more jobs than his counterpart who graduated from high school. These differences may result from differences in the age of school leaving across the three groups, or to differences in job turnover within groups.

The more interesting contrast looks at differences within each SLG by race/ethnicity. These differences are greatest for high school dropouts: White males on average have held more jobs at each age, and black males have held the fewest jobs. For example, at age 27, white male dropouts have held an average of 9.1 jobs, compared with 8.4 jobs for Hispanic males and 7.0 jobs for black males. These differences persist, as well, at the bottom and top of the jobs-held distribution. For the two other SLGs, blacks continue to accumulate fewer jobs at each age, while the distribution of jobs held for Hispanic and white males look virtually identical through the early-to-mid-twenties.[3]

How should we interpret these differences by race/ethnicity? Do these numbers indicate that whites mill about more in the labor market in their early career, while blacks have the most stable employment experiences? By viewing these numbers in light of the static analysis in Section 3, it is possible to conclude that black men hold fewer jobs not because they hold each job for a longer period, but because they spend more time unemployed or out of the labor force.[4] This issue will be explored further when we examine job durations in the "Timing of the Transition to Stable Employment" subsection.

---

[3]A similar pattern is reported by Veum and Weiss (1993) in their analysis of the average number of jobs held starting from age 18 by men and women in groups defined by completed schooling and race/ethnicity.

[4]Veum and Weiss (1993) report that black male dropouts have fewer weeks of work experience and more weeks of unemployment at each age between 18 and 27 compared with their white or Hispanic counterparts. A similar gap is evident for high school graduates, while the differences are almost eliminated for higher education groups. Their analysis, unlike ours, classifies youth by their completed schooling rather than SLG.

Table 4.2

Number of Jobs Held by Men, by School-Leaving Group, Race/Ethnicity, and Age, at Mean, and at 25th, 50th, and 75th Percentiles of Distribution

Age	N			Mean			25th Percentile			50th Percentile			75th Percentile		
	B	H	W	B	H	W	B	H	W	B	H	W	B	H	W
a. High school dropouts															
16	328	246	558	0.0	0.0	0.1	0	0	0	0	0	0	0	0	0
17	325	244	553	0.2	0.4	0.6	0	0	0	0	0	0	0	0	1
18	324	242	540	0.8	1.4	1.5	0	0	0	0	1	1	1	2	2
19	322	239	532	1.7	2.4	2.7	1	1	1	1	2	2	2	4	4
20	319	235	528	2.4	3.3	3.8	1	2	2	2	2	3	3	4	5
21	316	233	525	3.1	4.0	4.7	2	2	3	3	3	4	4	4	6
22	312	231	516	3.9	4.9	5.6	2	2	3	3	3	5	5	5	7
23	307	224	509	4.5	5.7	6.3	2	2	4	4	4	6	6	6	9
24	300	216	501	5.2	6.4	7.1	3	3	4	5	5	6	7	8	10
25	296	210	488	5.8	7.0	7.7	4	3	5	5	6	7	8	8	10
26	266	194	442	6.5	7.6	8.4	4	4	5	6	6	8	9	9	10
27	208	133	321	7.0	8.4	9.1	4	4	5	6	7	9	9	10	10
28	146	—	179	7.3	—	9.0	4	—	5	6	—	9	10	—	10
b. High school graduates															
16	373	158	696	0.0	0.0	0.0	0	0	0	0	0	0	0	0	0
17	372	158	695	0.0	0.0	0.0	0	0	0	0	0	0	0	0	0
18	368	157	692	0.3	0.4	0.4	0	0	0	0	0	0	0	1	1
19	363	155	684	1.1	1.4	1.6	0	1	1	1	1	1	2	2	2
20	362	153	678	2.0	2.3	2.6	1	1	1	2	2	2	3	3	3
21	358	153	668	2.7	3.2	3.4	2	1	2	2	3	3	4	4	5
22	356	151	661	3.3	3.8	4.2	2	2	2	3	3	4	4	5	6
23	354	149	657	4.0	4.4	4.8	2	2	3	4	4	4	5	6	6
24	347	146	650	4.6	4.9	5.5	3	2	3	4	5	5	6	7	7
25	339	144	642	5.2	5.4	6.0	3	3	3	5	5	5	7	7	8
26	317	134	584	5.8	5.8	6.5	3	3	3	5	5	6	8	8	9
27	246	115	456	6.2	6.4	6.8	4	3	3	6	6	6	8	9	9
28	185	—	334	6.8	—	7.3	4	—	4	7	—	6	9	—	10
29	118	—	207	7.5	—	7.7	4	—	4	7	—	7	10	—	10

Table 4.2—continued

c. Some college

Age	N B	N H	N W	Mean B	Mean H	Mean W	25th Percentile B	25th Percentile H	25th Percentile W	50th Percentile B	50th Percentile H	50th Percentile W	75th Percentile B	75th Percentile H	75th Percentile W
16	195	121	416	0.0	0.0	0.0	0	0	0	0	0	0	0	0	0
17	194	121	414	0.0	0.0	0.0	0	0	0	0	0	0	0	0	0
18	193	121	413	0.0	0.1	0.0	0	0	0	0	0	0	0	0	0
19	191	121	412	0.3	0.4	0.3	0	0	0	0	0	0	0	1	0
20	191	119	411	0.8	1.1	1.0	0	0	0	0	1	1	1	2	2
21	187	118	402	1.5	1.9	1.9	0	1	1	1	2	2	2	3	3
22	187	117	396	2.3	2.9	2.8	1	1	1	2	3	2	3	4	4
23	186	116	391	3.1	3.6	3.6	1	2	2	3	3	3	4	5	5
24	186	114	387	3.8	4.2	4.5	2	2	2	3	3	4	5	6	6
25	181	108	383	4.4	4.9	5.1	2	3	3	4	4	5	6	7	7
26	169	102	366	5.0	5.7	5.7	3	3	3	4	5	5	6	7	8
27	137	—	298	5.1	—	6.3	3	—	4	4	—	6	7	—	8
28	111	—	246	5.6	—	6.8	3	—	4	5	—	6	8	—	9

NOTES: B = black non-Hispanic, H = Hispanic, W = white non-Hispanic and other.
A value of 10 indicates 10 or more jobs.
N is the number of individuals in the sample at least through a given age. Results are shown when sample size for a given age-SLG-race/ethnic group combination exceeds 100.

Patterns for Women

Table 4.3 reports the mean number of jobs and distribution of the number of jobs for the NLS-Y women. Consistent with other studies (e.g., BLS, 1992; Veum and Weiss, 1993), the data reveal that women in the two lowest SLGs hold fewer jobs on average than men at each age. For example, at age 28, high school dropout men have accumulated nearly 1 additional job compared with women (8.6 versus 7.7 jobs); a similar gap exists for high school graduates (7.2 versus 6.3). The gap with men is smaller for those with some college, whereas college graduate women accumulate jobs more quickly compared with men in the same SLG.[5]

Compared with SLG differences between men, the differences between women in the four SLGs is smaller when viewed in terms of years since school leaving. For example, approximately six years after school leaving (at age 29), college graduate women have held 4.7 jobs. Women with some college and those who graduated from high school, who have approximately the same potential experience at age 26 and 25, respectively, have held 5.1 and 5.2 jobs on average, respectively. The dropout group at about the same point in the work history (at age 24) has held 5.7 jobs. Men in the same four SLGs (from dropouts to college graduates) at the same ages have held 6.7, 5.9, 5.6, and 3.8 jobs, respectively, a gap of nearly 3 jobs between the dropouts and college graduates. Within each SLG, there is less heterogeneity among women than among men, as seen by the narrower spread between the number of jobs held at the 25th versus the 75th percentile.

Timing of the Transition to Stable Employment

The results on the number of jobs held suggest a considerable amount of milling about—i.e., not holding any job for very long. For a given number of years since school leaving, the amount of milling about is lower for those in the higher schooling groups. Within each SLG, the number of jobs held is almost always higher for whites than for blacks, and, sometimes, than for Hispanics. These differences could indicate either shorter job durations for young white men or, alternatively, more time spent out of work for young black men. Likewise, while women who left school at the same point typically hold fewer jobs on average when compared with men at each age, it is not clear that this difference indicates a more stable transition in the early career. To explore this issue further, we

---

[5]When only full-time jobs are counted, college graduate women hold fewer jobs on average at each age than men in the same SLG.

Table 4.3

Number of Jobs Held by Women, by School-Leaving Group and Age, at Mean, and at 25th, 50th, and 75th Percentiles of Distribution

Age	N				HSDO				HSG				SC				CG			
	HSDO	HSG	SC	CG	Mean	25th	50th	75th	Mean	25th	50th	75th	Mean	25th	50th	75th	Mean	25th	50th	75th
17	812	1306	1000	378	0.5	0	0	1	0.0	0	0	0	0.0	0	0	0	0.0	0	0	0
18	803	1301	999	377	1.3	0	1	2	0.5	0	0	1	0.0	0	0	0	0.0	0	0	0
19	793	1290	995	376	2.1	1	2	3	1.5	1	1	2	0.3	0	0	0	0.0	0	0	0
20	786	1277	991	374	3.0	1	3	4	2.4	1	2	3	0.9	0	1	1	0.0	0	0	0
21	782	1267	986	374	3.8	2	3	5	3.1	2	3	4	1.7	0	1	2	0.1	0	0	0
22	776	1253	978	370	4.5	2	4	6	3.6	2	3	5	2.5	1	2	4	0.7	0	0	1
23	769	1236	967	367	5.1	3	5	7	4.2	2	4	6	3.3	2	3	4	1.7	1	1	2
24	760	1222	955	364	5.7	3	5	8	4.7	3	4	6	3.9	2	3	5	2.4	1	2	3
25	747	1198	940	359	6.2	4	6	8	5.2	3	5	7	4.5	2	4	6	2.9	1	2	4
26	698	1121	903	348	6.8	4	6	9	5.6	3	5	7	5.1	3	4	7	3.4	2	3	5
27	500	877	783	309	7.3	4	6	10	6.0	3	6	8	5.5	3	5	7	3.8	2	3	5
28	302	613	660	272	7.7	5	7	10	6.3	4	6	9	5.9	3	5	8	4.3	2	4	6
29	—	366	529	236	—	—	—	—	6.5	4	7	9	6.3	4	5	8	4.7	2	4	6
30	—	171	365	184	—	—	—	—	6.2	4	7	10	6.4	4	6	8	4.9	3	4	8
31	—	—	222	—	—	—	—	—	—	—	—	—	6.4	4	6	9	—	—	—	—

NOTES: A value of 10 indicates 10 or more jobs.

N is the number of individuals in the sample at least through a given age. Results are shown when sample size for a given age-SLG combination exceeds 150.

continue our dynamic analysis by examining the time since school leaving when young men and women first hold a job lasting one, two, or three years.

We view the experience of holding a job for one to three years as one useful measure of the concept of *stable employment*. It is the opposite of milling about. While we do not evaluate whether these are "good jobs" on the basis of compensation or potential for career advancement, tenure on the job is one measure of the process of settling down and a possible indicator of the transition to a career job. We also examine the sensitivity of our results to alternative definitions of *job duration* that have been used in the literature.

Patterns for Men

Figures 4.1, 4.2, and 4.3 plot, for each year since school leaving, the percentage of men at each age ever in a job that lasted one, two, or three years, respectively. For example, five years after school leaving, Figure 4.3 shows that about 21 percent of high school dropouts have ever held a job that lasted three years, whereas 55 percent of college graduates have done so. About one-third of those in the high school graduate and some college groups have achieved the same status.

This general pattern exists for each measure of job duration. In all cases, measuring time from school leaving, those in the college graduate group make the transition to stable employment fastest; high school dropouts make the transition the slowest. In the middle are male high school graduates and those with some college. The behavior of these latter two groups (as measured by time since leaving school) is nearly indistinguishable.

The preceding figures have plotted the transition to stable employment by time since school leaving. Figures 4.4, 4.5, and 4.6 and Table 4.4 display the same information by the age of the individual. Shortly after school leaving, the age at school leaving dominates these figures: High school dropouts are in the labor market for the longest period of time, so they have more time to experience a job lasting one, two, or three years. This effect wears off quite quickly. Within a year or two after it is chronologically possible, high school graduates overtake high school dropouts in terms of the percentage who have ever held a job for one, two, or three years. By age 30, college graduates rise to the level of the other three groups. For longer jobs, college graduates overtake those with some college and dropouts within a year or two of the first possible time (i.e., four or five years after they enter the labor market). While those with some college eventually

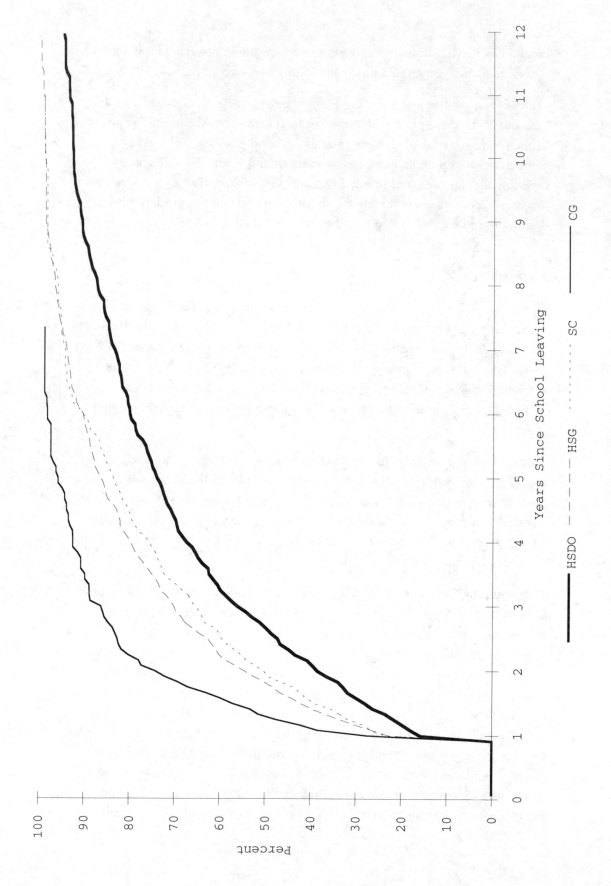

Figure 4.1—Percentage of Men Ever in a Job 1 or More Years, by Years Since School Leaving

49

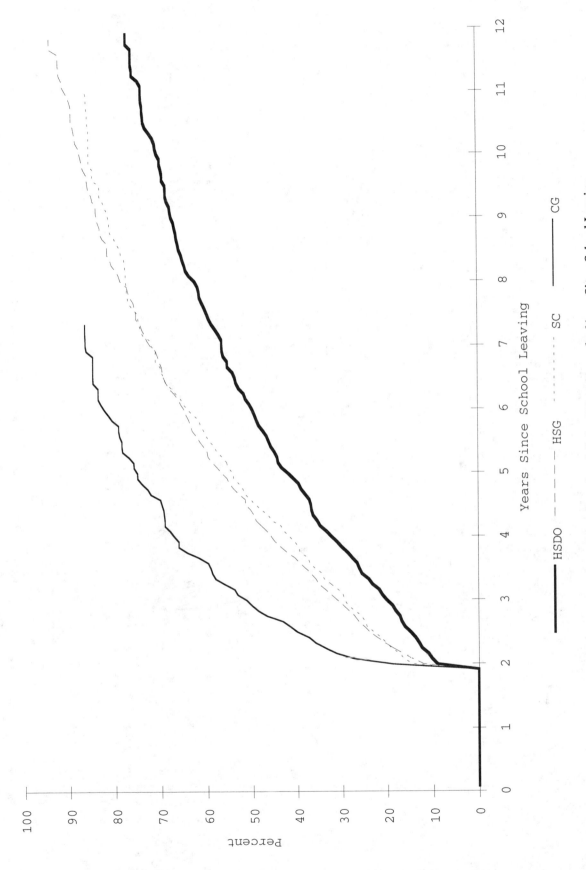

HSDO ————   HSG – – – –   SC ···········   CG —————

Years Since School Leaving

Percent

Figure 4.2—Percentage of Men Ever in a Job 2 or More Years, by Years Since School Leaving

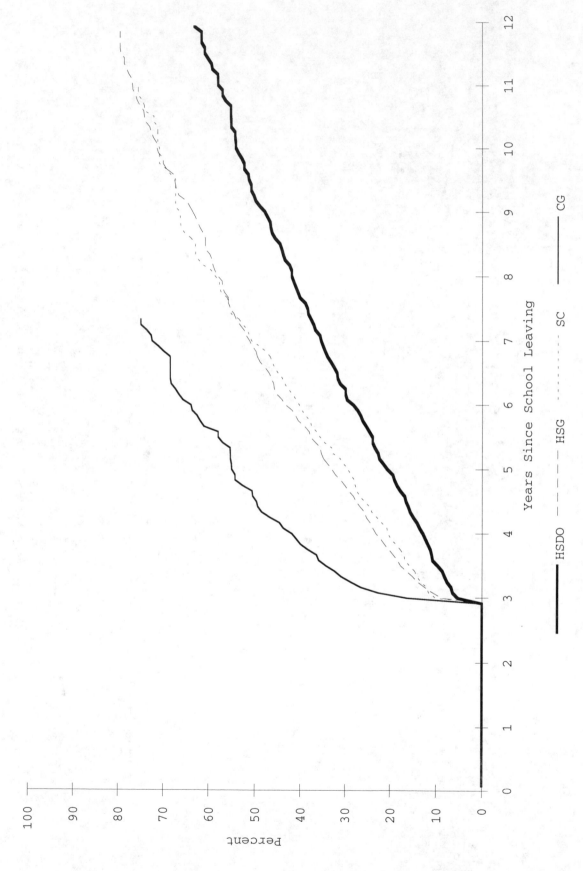

Figure 4.3—Percentage of Men Ever in a Job 3 or More Years, by Years Since School Leaving

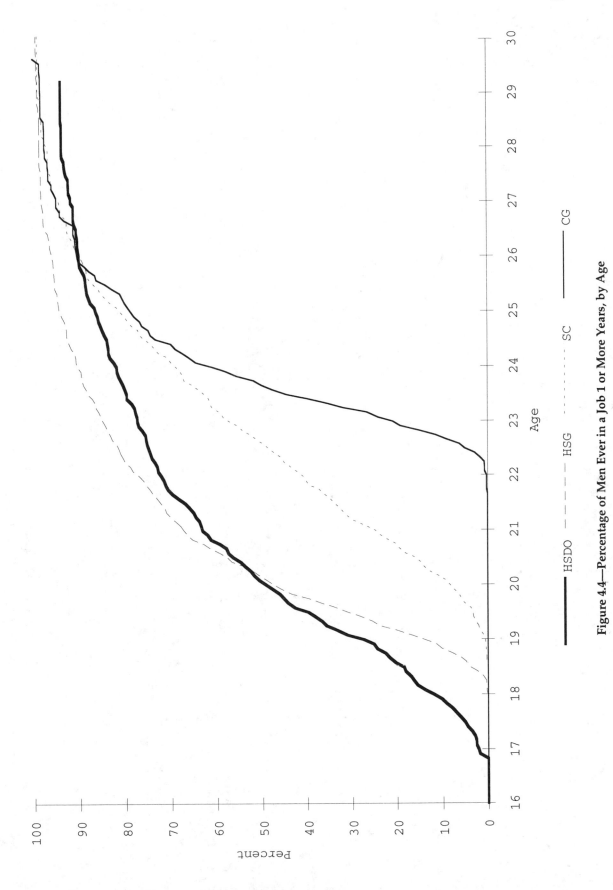

Figure 4.4—Percentage of Men Ever in a Job 1 or More Years, by Age

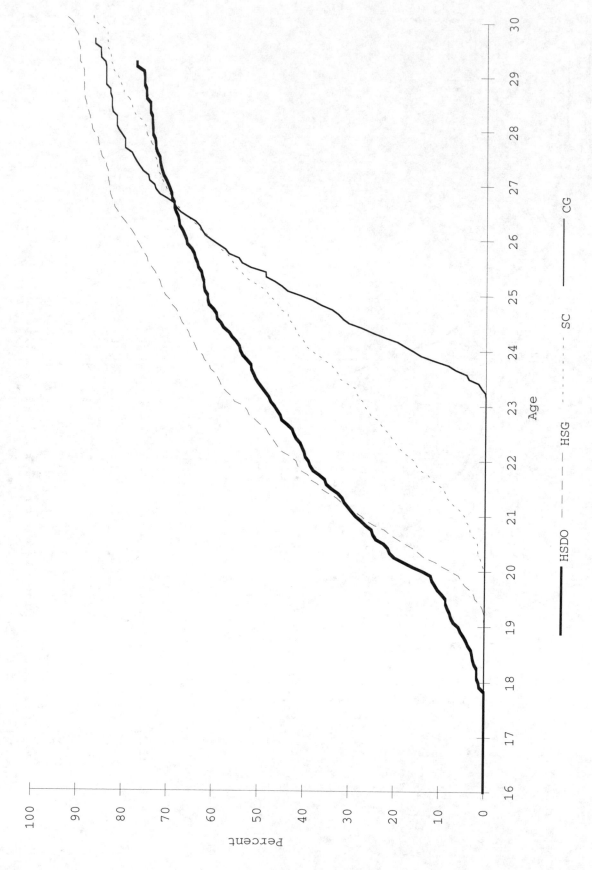

Figure 4.5—Percentage of Men Ever in a Job 2 or More Years, by Age

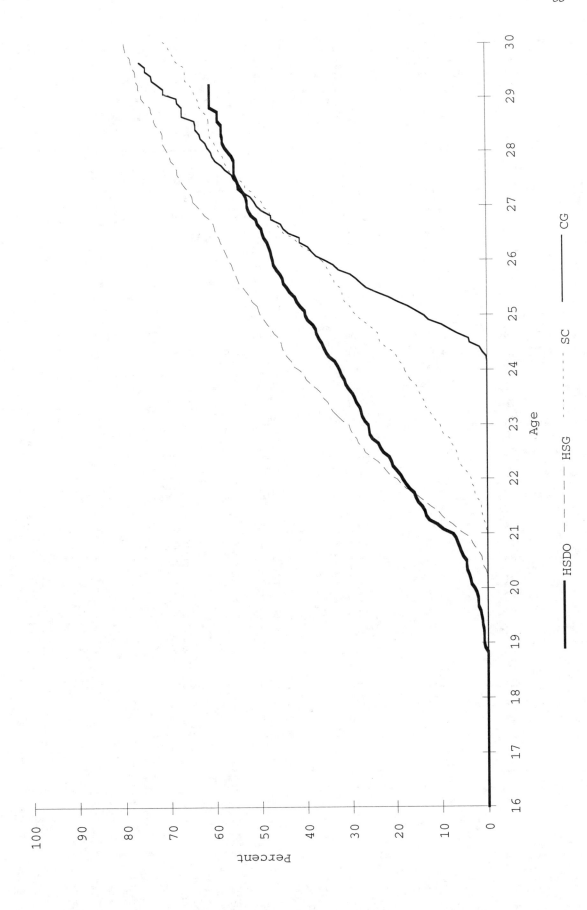

Figure 4.6—Percentage of Men Ever in a Job 3 or More Years, by Age

Table 4.4

**Percentage of Men, by School-Leaving Group and Age,
Ever in a Job 1, 2, and 3 Years**

Age	N	Duration of Longest Job Ever Held		
		1 Year	2 Years	3 Years
		a. High school dropouts		
16	1132	0.0	0.0	0.0
17	1122	2.1	0.0	0.0
18	1106	11.9	1.2	0.0
19	1093	27.5	5.7	0.8
20	1082	49.0	13.7	2.8
21	1074	63.2	28.6	7.5
22	1059	72.2	39.1	18.4
23	1040	77.4	46.6	26.0
24	1017	81.9	54.1	32.4
25	994	86.4	61.4	40.1
26	902	90.0	66.2	47.1
27	662	91.8	70.3	52.7
28	413	93.7	73.7	56.8
29	194	93.8	75.6	60.8
		b. High school graduates		
16	1227	0.0	0.0	0.0
17	1225	0.0	0.0	0.0
18	1217	0.1	0.0	0.0
19	1202	14.2	0.1	0.0
20	1193	47.3	7.3	0.1
21	1179	67.4	27.4	5.2
22	1168	77.1	41.8	19.7
23	1160	84.9	53.4	30.5
24	1143	90.5	63.7	41.3
25	1125	94.3	70.9	49.9
26	1035	95.9	77.4	57.0
27	817	98.2	83.4	63.6
28	598	98.6	87.1	70.1
29	376	99.0	89.0	75.7
30	183	99.2	91.7	79.5

Table 4.4—continued

		Duration of Longest Job Ever Held		
Age	N	1 year	2 years	3 years
		c. Some college		
16	732	0.0	0.0	0.0
17	729	0.0	0.0	0.0
18	727	0.0	0.0	0.0
19	724	0.6	0.0	0.0
20	721	8.4	0.0	0.0
21	707	24.8	4.5	0.0
22	700	41.0	15.6	3.6
23	693	57.3	26.8	10.2
24	687	69.1	38.6	17.9
25	672	81.2	48.0	28.8
26	637	89.8	61.0	36.3
27	517	94.3	71.1	49.4
28	425	96.7	75.2	58.8
29	323	98.9	81.6	63.5
30	228	98.9	86.9	70.2
31	156	99.1	87.5	76.8
		d. College graduates		
16	309	0.0	0.0	0.0
17	307	0.0	0.0	0.0
18	307	0.0	0.0	0.0
19	306	0.0	0.0	0.0
20	304	0.0	0.0	0.0
21	303	0.0	0.0	0.0
22	301	0.2	0.0	0.0
23	297	20.8	0.0	0.0
24	295	61.1	16.0	0.0
25	294	78.8	40.9	13.6
26	279	90.4	60.7	35.4
27	242	94.9	73.4	50.5
28	205	97.4	81.3	60.6
29	169	98.2	84.1	68.0

NOTES: N is the number of individuals in the sample at least through a given age. Results are shown when sample size for a given age-SLG combination exceeds 150.

overtake high school dropouts, through age 30 they tend to lag behind high school graduates.

For college graduates, there is relatively little variability in the timing of the transition to stable employment. The median male college graduate holds a job for one year before his 24th birthday, a job for two years before his 26th birthday, and a job for three years before his 27th birthday (see panel d of Table 4.4). A college graduate male at the 25th percentile of the duration distribution also holds his job lasting one year before age 24, and essentially stays with that job, progressing to each later cutoff (two years and three years) about a year later. Just before age 25, a college graduate male at the 75th percentile holds a job for one year. He takes three more years to stay in a job two years, and has not stayed in a job three years by age 29, when the data become too sparse for analysis. The pattern for the median male with some college is similar to that for the median college graduate. There is more heterogeneity because of the variation in date of leaving school and the fact that some people return to school.

At the other extreme, despite the fact that he usually entered the labor force before his 17th birthday, the median male dropout does not hold a job for a year until just after his 20th birthday (see panel a of Table 4.4). The median dropout does not reach the 2-year- and 3-year-tenure points until ages 23 and 26, respectively. This implies that the median dropout did not enter a job lasting one, two, and three years until he was 19, 21, and 23, respectively.[6] For high school dropouts, the variance is substantial. At the 25th percentile of the job-duration distribution, dropouts reach the 1-, 2-, and 3-year-tenure points before ages 19, 21, and 23, a pace that is faster than that of the median high school graduates. Dropouts at the 75th percentile do not reach the 1-year-tenure point until age 22, and the 2-year-tenure point is just reached by age 29, when the data become too sparse for further analysis.

Finally, we turn to the pattern for high school graduates, the focus of the frequently cited stylized facts concerning the school-to-work transition. The median high school graduate has held a job for at least one year by the time he turns 21, two years by the time he turns 23, and three years by the time he turns 26 (see panel b of Table 4.4). Subtracting the time required to achieve each job tenure, we conclude that the median male high school graduate entered a job that

---

[6]This computation proceeds by noting that if more than 50 percent of all people in an SLG have been in a job M years by the birthday when they turned A years, then the median person reached that point when he was $A - 1$ years old, and he entered the job at least $A - 1 - M$ years earlier. So, for example, reading from Table 4.4, the high school dropout percentiles for 2 years' job tenure are 46.6 and 54.1 at the birthdays at which the young men turned 23 and 24, respectively. Thus, the median male reached his 2-year-tenure date while he was 23 and had entered a job that would eventually last at least two years by the time he was 21.

would last one, two, and three years by the time he was 19, 20, and 22, respectively.[7]

If holding a job for two or even three years is not "milling about," then the patterns in Table 4.4 do not support the impression conveyed in the CSAW (1990) report that the typical high school student mills about in the labor market until age 23 or 24. It is true that the median high school graduate does not settle immediately into a long-tenure job. However, characterizing the settling-down process as lasting into the mid-twenties (e.g., 24 or 25) is overly pessimistic for the typical male in that group.

We reach this conclusion for a group of high school graduate men that includes those who returned to school full time (nearly 30 percent of the sample). If we exclude those who returned to school, the median transition to stable employment occurs somewhat earlier (see Appendix C). For example, the median high school graduate who never returned to school first enters a 3-year-tenure job at age 21 versus age 22 for his counterpart at the median of the group who ever returned to school.

While this is the pattern for the median high school graduate, the experience varies considerably at the extremes of the distribution. At the 25th percentile, high school graduates entered the 1-, 2-, and 3-year jobs while they were 18, 18, and 19 years old, respectively—that is, from one to three years ahead of the median. This probably describes what is possible in the U.S. system for young men with "successful" transitions. At the 75th percentile, young male high school graduates experienced a school-to-work transition that corresponds more closely to the perception noted at the beginning of the report. At that point in the distribution, graduates entered the 1-, 2-, and 3-year jobs at 20, 23, and 25, respectively. These transitions correspond more closely to the portrait conveyed in the CSAW (1990) report.

A Sensitivity Analysis

These results provide a considerably brighter picture of the school-to-work transition than has been presented elsewhere in the literature using the same data (see, for example, Osterman and Iannozzi, 1993). The difference derives primarily from different methods of summarizing dynamic labor market data. We define "milling about" as ending *permanently* when a young person *first* enters a job that will ultimately last more than M years. In our discussion, we

---

[7]See footnote 6 for the computation.

58

subtracted M years from the age at which we observed that the individual has been in the job M years. We then considered the resulting age (the age at which he or she first entered the job that would last M years) as the end of "milling about." At least two other concepts are possible. First, we could ask whether or not the job a person is *currently* in *has lasted* or *will last* at least M years. Second, we can ask whether the current job has *already lasted* at least M years (Osterman and Iannozzi, 1993, employ this last definition).

For high school graduate men, Table 4.5 (panel b) compares the results from these differing concepts as of the time a person is exactly a given age (on each birthday) for job durations of one, two, and three years. (For purposes of comparison, Table 4.5 also presents results for the three other SLGs. The qualitative results are similar.) For each age and job duration, we present three numbers corresponding to the three concepts just described. The column labeled "L" corresponds to the *longest* job a person has ever held as of the given age (our preferred definition). The column labeled "E" corresponds to the *eventual* length of the current job at that age. The column labeled "C" corresponds to the length to date of the *current* job at that age. There is a formal relation between these concepts. The current job duration is always less than or equal to the eventual duration of the job, which is always less than or equal to the duration of the longest job M years later (i.e., M rows down the table in the "L" column).

According to Table 4.5, the tenure on the current job clearly gives the most negative results (column C). Consider, for example, the 2-year-duration job as of age 26 for high school graduate men (panel b of Table 4.5). More than half of all high school graduates at age 26, 54.6 percent (100.0 – 45.4), have not been in their current job for even two years. Note, however, that for nearly half, 46.5 percent [(70.8 – 45.4)/54.6], of those people whose current job has not lasted two years, the current job itself will last two years. Further, nearly one-quarter, 22.6 percent [(77.4 – 70.8)/(100.0 – 70.8)], of the men whose current job will not last two years have already held a job that has lasted two years. Put differently, half of all high school graduates at a given age are *not* in a job that will last two years until nearly age 27. However, just after his 21st birthday, the median high school graduate is in a job that *will last* at least two years. Finally, before his 20th birthday, the median high school graduate has, at some earlier point in his work history (perhaps not the current job), entered a job that eventually lasted at least two years.

Following our earlier discussion of the literature on job matching (e.g., Mincer and Jovanovic, 1981; Flinn, 1986; McCall, 1990), we are reluctant to view all job turnover as bad. The literature on job matching suggests that most job changes

Table 4.5

**Percentage of Men, by School-Leaving Group, with Job Tenure of
1, 2, and 3 Years Under Different Job-Tenure Concepts**

Age	N	1 Year			2 Years			3 Years		
		L	E	C	L	E	C	L	E	C
				a. High school dropouts						
16	1132	0.0	1.8	0.0	0.0	1.0	0.0	0.0	0.5	0.0
17	1122	2.1	10.2	2.1	0.0	5.2	0.0	0.0	2.4	0.0
18	1106	11.9	23.0	9.0	1.2	11.9	1.2	0.0	6.8	0.0
19	1093	27.5	39.7	15.0	5.7	25.7	3.5	0.8	17.3	0.6
20	1082	49.0	49.1	28.5	13.7	34.5	8.0	2.8	24.2	1.3
21	1074	63.2	52.1	34.5	28.6	38.5	18.2	7.5	29.7	5.0
22	1059	72.2	57.8	36.4	39.1	43.4	22.8	18.4	35.4	13.0
23	1040	77.4	61.1	40.7	46.6	47.7	23.9	26.0	38.5	15.0
24	1017	81.9	64.3	44.3	54.1	49.3	27.2	32.4	40.9	17.0
25	994	86.4	67.0	46.3	61.4	50.3	30.5	40.1	40.5	19.9
26	902	90.0	65.8	46.6	66.2	51.0	31.3	47.1	42.0	22.8
27	662	91.8	70.2	47.3	70.3	57.2	33.4	52.7	46.8	25.3
28	413	93.7	68.1	50.3	73.7	58.4	33.2	56.8	48.5	25.5
29	194	93.8	72.0	58.4	75.6	—	43.5	60.8	—	27.2
				b. High school graduates						
16	1227	0.0	0.0	0.0	0.0	0.0	0.0	0.0	0.0	0.0
17	1225	0.0	0.1	0.0	0.0	0.1	0.0	0.0	0.1	0.0
18	1217	0.1	11.5	0.1	0.0	5.7	0.0	0.0	3.7	0.0
19	1202	14.2	44.2	11.6	0.1	26.0	0.1	0.0	18.5	0.0
20	1193	47.3	59.1	34.2	7.3	40.7	6.5	0.1	29.8	0.1
21	1179	67.4	63.7	42.4	27.4	49.0	21.5	5.2	39.5	4.3
22	1168	77.1	66.1	45.3	41.8	54.8	28.0	19.7	46.0	15.5
23	1160	84.9	75.2	52.2	53.4	60.4	34.1	30.5	50.0	21.4
24	1143	90.5	74.5	54.7	63.7	62.7	37.5	41.3	53.0	25.9
25	1125	94.3	78.7	58.1	70.9	67.1	41.4	49.9	58.6	30.7
26	1035	95.9	81.0	61.3	77.4	70.8	45.4	57.0	63.5	33.8
27	817	98.2	86.4	66.8	83.4	76.0	51.1	63.6	67.3	39.1
28	598	98.6	85.2	68.8	87.1	76.2	53.4	70.1	67.1	42.9
29	376	99.0	85.6	66.8	89.0	76.2	52.0	75.7	68.7	44.3
30	183	99.2	91.2	73.3	91.7	—	56.1	79.5	—	45.8

Table 4.5—continued

Age	N	1 Year			2 Years			3 Years		
		L	E	C	L	E	C	L	E	C
				c. Some college						
16	732	0.0	0.0	0.0	0.0	0.0	0.0	0.0	0.0	0.0
17	729	0.0	0.0	0.0	0.0	0.0	0.0	0.0	0.0	0.0
18	727	0.0	0.5	0.0	0.0	0.0	0.0	0.0	0.0	0.0
19	724	0.6	7.4	0.4	0.0	4.2	0.0	0.0	3.5	0.0
20	721	8.4	23.0	6.3	0.0	15.0	0.0	0.0	9.7	0.0
21	707	24.8	35.5	17.5	4.5	25.4	4.1	0.0	17.0	0.0
22	700	41.0	48.1	25.6	15.6	34.3	11.8	3.6	27.2	3.4
23	693	57.3	57.5	37.4	26.8	41.4	17.7	10.2	33.7	8.3
24	687	69.1	67.6	42.0	38.6	51.4	25.2	17.9	42.7	12.9
25	672	81.2	76.4	50.3	48.0	60.1	29.9	28.8	50.8	20.0
26	637	89.8	81.3	59.0	61.0	64.6	36.5	36.3	54.8	21.3
27	517	94.3	81.4	59.6	71.1	69.6	43.7	49.4	59.2	28.9
28	425	96.7	86.0	64.7	75.2	73.1	45.8	58.8	63.5	34.0
29	323	98.9	84.5	66.8	81.6	75.0	48.8	63.5	67.8	36.6
30	228	98.9	80.8	64.4	86.9	72.3	52.2	70.2	66.1	38.3
31	156	99.1	—	69.5	87.5	—	53.6	76.8	—	45.2
				d. College graduates						
16	309	0.0	0.0	0.0	0.0	0.0	0.0	0.0	0.0	0.0
17	307	0.0	0.0	0.0	0.0	0.0	0.0	0.0	0.0	0.0
18	307	0.0	0.0	0.0	0.0	0.0	0.0	0.0	0.0	0.0
19	306	0.0	0.0	0.0	0.0	0.0	0.0	0.0	0.0	0.0
20	304	0.0	0.0	0.0	0.0	0.0	0.0	0.0	0.0	0.0
21	303	0.0	0.2	0.0	0.0	0.0	0.0	0.0	0.0	0.0
22	301	0.2	18.9	0.0	0.0	14.2	0.0	0.0	12.4	0.0
23	297	20.8	56.5	18.3	0.0	38.2	0.0	0.0	33.0	0.0
24	295	61.1	73.2	47.6	16.0	59.2	15.8	0.0	48.8	0.0
25	294	78.8	85.3	58.9	40.9	71.3	35.9	13.6	60.4	12.6
26	279	90.4	85.2	68.9	60.7	75.3	48.6	35.4	66.7	31.5
27	242	94.9	89.7	70.5	73.4	79.8	55.4	50.5	73.0	43.1
28	205	97.4	84.3	68.9	81.3	77.2	54.0	60.6	72.2	43.5
29	169	98.2	88.8	68.2	84.1	81.1	59.0	68.0	79.5	49.1

NOTES: Statistics are as of the birthday in the age column.

N   The number of individuals in the sample at least through the given age. Cells are empty when there are less than 150 observations. Note that to compute "E," whether the current job will last at least M years, we need to be able to observe the person for another M years. Thus, some cells in the E column are empty.

L   Longest job ever held lasted at least M years.

E   Current job will eventually last at least M years.

C   Current job has already lasted at least M years.

involve sizable wage increases. From this perspective, we are concerned about measures of employment stability that consider to be a poor outcome (i.e., an indication of an unsuccessful transition to stable employment)[8] those individuals who have not, at an arbitrary point in time, been in their *current* job for several years. A similar criticism applies to definitions that consider the eventual duration of the current job.

Nevertheless, we agree that in and of itself, failure to stay on a job for a significant period of time (one, two, or even three years) often indicates some problem. If employers do not expect young workers to stay on the job even for such a moderate period of time, they will not invest in even the minimal training required for primary-sector jobs. However, a worker who spends several years at one employer and then moves on to a new job (often with a large increase in pay) is not a failure: The new job could also last several years.

Even a short job (under a year) between two longer jobs need not be a failure. Perhaps the short job did not "work out"; perhaps it was deliberately temporary until an appropriate career-enhancing job became available (perhaps the worker had already lined up that next good job). For all these reasons, we prefer our definition of *transition period* as the time until the young worker first enters a job that will eventually last more than M years. And, again for the same reasons, we are concerned that the alternative definitions we have discussed present an overly pessimistic view of labor market dynamics.

Differences by Race/Ethnicity

The analysis for all young men indicated that there is considerable variation across SLGs in the timing of the transition to stable employment. Further, there is heterogeneity within these groups as evidenced by differences in the experiences of the typical male versus those who make the transition more rapidly or more slowly. We would like to know if there is variation, as well, among men in different race/ethnic groups. To address this question, in Table 4.6 we report the percentage of black, Hispanic, and white men within each SLG who have held a job of one, two, and three years' duration at each age. For the 2-year-duration job, Figures 4.7, 4.8, and 4.9 plot the percentage of men in each of

---

[8]This distinction—time in a job at an interview versus completed job duration—is discussed for the case of job tenure in Horvath (1982), which is based on a discussion in the unemployment literature (Bowers, 1980).

Table 4.6

Percentage of Men, by School-Leaving Group, Race/Ethnicity, and Age, Ever in a Job 1, 2, and 3 Years

Age	N			1 Year			2 Years			3 Years		
	B	H	W	B	H	W	B	H	W	B	H	W
				a. High school dropouts								
16	328	246	558	0.0	0.0	0.0	0.0	0.0	0.0	0.0	0.0	0.0
17	325	244	553	1.4	1.3	2.4	0.0	0.0	0.0	0.0	0.0	0.0
18	324	242	540	7.6	9.1	13.4	1.0	0.0	1.5	0.0	0.0	0.0
19	322	239	532	18.4	26.1	29.9	3.7	4.8	6.3	0.4	0.0	1.0
20	319	235	528	37.1	45.1	52.5	10.4	11.9	14.8	2.5	2.3	3.0
21	316	233	525	52.3	59.4	66.4	21.8	26.4	30.6	6.9	5.3	8.0
22	312	231	516	62.8	66.1	75.3	32.7	36.8	41.0	13.7	15.9	19.9
23	307	224	509	69.1	71.6	80.2	39.2	43.7	48.8	22.3	21.8	27.5
24	300	216	501	76.0	75.6	84.2	45.1	50.5	56.8	28.3	26.7	34.1
25	296	210	488	81.2	81.9	88.3	50.6	61.4	64.1	32.4	32.7	42.9
26	266	194	442	83.0	85.9	92.3	55.3	66.7	68.8	38.7	43.2	49.7
27	208	133	321	85.7	89.8	93.6	56.5	70.9	73.7	42.7	48.5	55.7
28	146	—	179	88.2	—	95.3	57.9	—	77.6	43.1	—	60.8
				b. High school graduates								
16	373	158	696	0.0	0.0	0.0	0.0	0.0	0.0	0.0	0.0	0.0
17	372	158	695	0.0	0.0	0.0	0.0	0.0	0.0	0.0	0.0	0.0
18	368	157	692	0.4	0.5	0.0	0.0	0.0	0.0	0.0	0.0	0.0
19	363	155	684	9.9	19.3	14.7	0.4	0.5	0.0	0.0	0.0	0.0
20	362	153	678	35.2	51.1	49.3	5.5	12.9	7.4	0.4	0.0	0.0
21	358	153	668	56.5	69.7	69.3	22.5	29.8	28.1	4.0	8.1	5.2
22	356	151	661	70.3	77.5	78.4	39.7	42.9	42.2	18.2	21.6	19.8
23	354	149	657	78.0	87.4	86.1	50.2	52.0	54.1	32.2	32.1	30.1
24	347	146	650	84.2	91.5	91.6	57.3	62.0	65.0	40.7	43.8	41.3
25	339	144	642	89.3	95.0	95.1	64.1	73.9	72.0	47.2	50.7	50.4
26	317	134	584	92.6	97.3	96.5	69.1	77.7	78.9	53.3	58.0	57.6
27	246	115	456	94.7	97.8	98.8	75.1	84.1	84.8	58.1	62.3	64.7
28	185	—	334	95.3	—	99.1	79.6	—	88.7	63.4	—	71.5
29	118	—	207	96.0	—	99.6	82.7	—	90.4	65.4	—	78.0

Table 4.6—continued

c. Some college

Age	N			1 Year			2 Years			3 Years		
	B	H	W	B	H	W	B	H	W	B	H	W
16	195	121	416	0.0	0.0	0.0	0.0	0.0	0.0	0.0	0.0	0.0
17	194	121	414	0.0	0.0	0.0	0.0	0.0	0.0	0.0	0.0	0.0
18	193	121	413	0.0	0.0	0.0	0.0	0.0	0.0	0.0	0.0	0.0
19	191	121	412	0.6	0.9	0.6	0.0	0.0	0.0	0.0	0.0	0.0
20	191	119	411	8.7	14.8	7.8	0.2	0.0	0.0	0.0	0.0	0.0
21	187	118	402	21.0	30.3	25.0	3.4	7.6	4.4	0.2	0.0	0.0
22	187	117	396	37.2	46.6	41.2	10.7	19.1	16.2	3.4	3.7	3.6
23	186	116	391	59.0	61.6	56.7	22.2	29.2	27.3	8.0	13.5	10.4
24	186	114	387	69.0	70.7	69.0	40.5	45.1	37.7	17.0	22.7	17.8
25	181	108	383	78.8	80.3	81.6	47.9	55.0	47.4	32.9	35.3	27.6
26	169	102	366	86.6	86.2	90.6	55.3	63.4	61.7	36.7	43.8	35.7
27	137	—	298	89.6	—	95.1	67.2	—	71.7	45.0	—	49.9
28	111	—	246	92.3	—	97.5	73.5	—	75.1	53.0	—	59.5

NOTES: B = black non-Hispanic, H = Hispanic, W = white non-Hispanic and other.
N is the number of individuals in the sample at least through a given age. Results are shown when sample size for a given age-SLG-race/ethnic group combination exceeds 100.

64

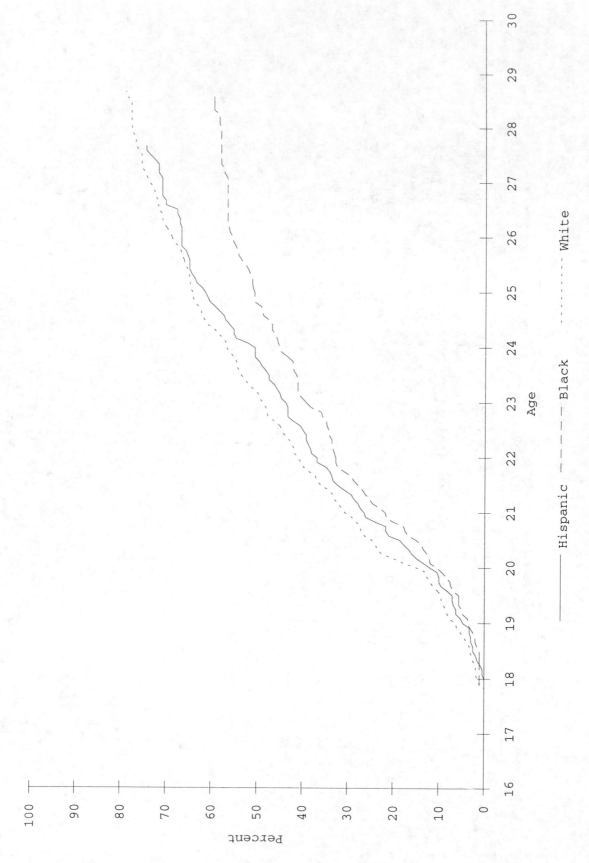

Figure 4.7—Percentage of High School Dropout Men Ever in a Job 2 or More Years, by Age

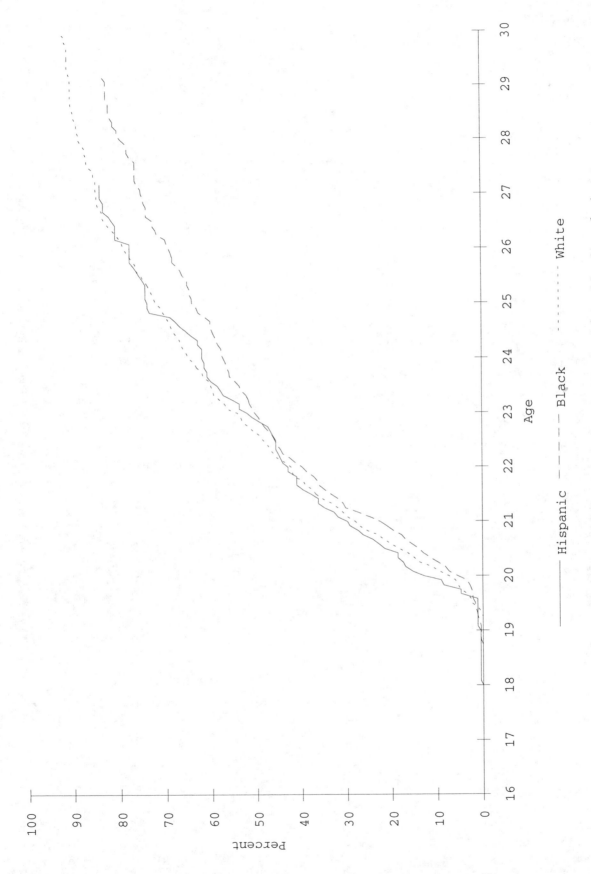

Figure 4.8—Percentage of High School Graduate Men Ever in a Job 2 or More Years, by Age

Hispanic ——— Black - - - - - White · · · · · ·

65

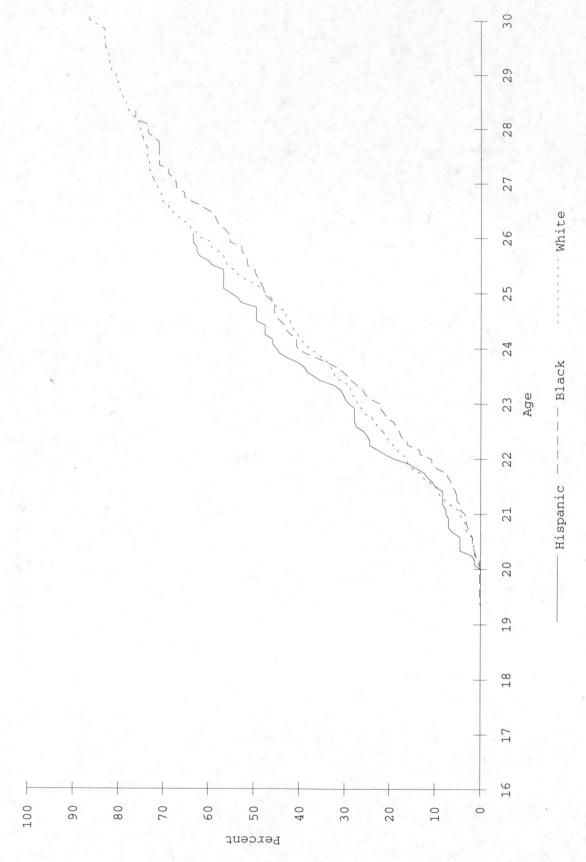

Figure 4.9—Percentage of Men with Some College Ever in a Job 2 or More Years, by Age

three groups—high school dropouts, high school graduates, and those with some college, respectively[9]—attaining this status.

While there is considerable heterogeneity between and within SLGs, there is surprisingly little variation in the distribution of job durations for men of different race/ethnicity within each SLG. Focusing on Figures 4.8 and 4.9, we find it hard to distinguish between the experience of white, black, and Hispanic high school graduates or those with some college. At each age with sufficient data to make a comparison, the fraction who had held a job for at least two years is similar for all three groups. The median black and white males with some college, for example, each had held a job for at least two years before their 26th birthday; the median Hispanic male had reached this status in the months before turning 25.

Among high school graduates, more diversity is indicated in the experience among black males than that among their white and Hispanic counterparts. Although the lines in Figure 4.8 track each other closely until age 23, they diverge somewhat after that point. This divergence can be viewed in terms of the differential experience of men at the 50th versus the 75th percentile of the distribution. For each of the three groups, the median high school graduate has held a job with at least two years of tenure before turning 23. In contrast, the white male high school graduate at the 75th percentile reaches a job with 2-year tenure before turning 26, and the Hispanic male at the same point in his distribution reaches this status several months earlier. The black male high school graduate at the 75th percentile has not held a job for two years until just before his 27th birthday. Thus, while the typical (i.e., at the 50th percentile) white, black, and Hispanic high school graduates show a similar transition to stable employment, at the tails of the distribution, black males make the transition more slowly.

Although the patterns are largely similar among high school graduates and men with some college, differences among black, Hispanic, and white male high school dropouts are considerably more pronounced. They are evident in Figure 4.7, which shows that black male dropouts make the transition to stable employment at a slower pace than Hispanic or white male dropouts. While there is evidence that Hispanic men lag behind their white counterparts, the differences between these two groups are not as sharp as the contrast with the pattern for black dropouts. For example, the median white and Hispanic males have held a job for a least two years by the time they reach 24, whereas this status

---

[9]The sample sizes become too small for a comparison by race/ethnicity within the college graduate group.

is not attained by black dropouts until more than one year later. A similar pattern is evident for the 1-year-tenure job, and will also hold for the 3-year-tenure job (for which the pattern must be inferred after age 28).

The patterns among race/ethnic groups in the transition to stable employment are surprising in light of the preceding results regarding the number of jobs held early in the career. Recall, for example, that white high school dropouts at each age held more jobs on average than their Hispanic counterparts, who in turn held more jobs than black high school dropouts. This result, however, does not translate into a more difficult transition to stable employment for white men. In fact, the reverse is true: A higher fraction of white high school dropouts has held a job for at least two years at each age compared with black dropouts. Likewise, the higher number of jobs held on average by white or Hispanic high school graduates (and those with some college) compared with blacks does not result in large differences between the race/ethnic groups in the timing of the transition to stable employment.

It is possible to reconcile the results of the analysis of the number of jobs held with our findings on job durations. If black men are more likely to experience spells between jobs, during which they are in school, unemployed, or out of the labor force, they will hold fewer jobs as they make the transition to stable employment. Conversely, if white and Hispanic men are more likely to make transitions from job to job, with many jobs lasting for only a short duration, they will hold more jobs in their early career. The static analysis in Section 3 supports this hypothesis: Black men, especially dropouts, are much more likely at any point in time to be unemployed or not in the labor force. Thus, it is unlikely that variation in the propensity to return to school can explain the racial differences we observed. We leave reconciling these dynamic differentials to subsequent work.

Patterns for Women

Consistent with our earlier analyses, the patterns for women vary in a number of ways from those evident for men. Table 4.7 shows the percentage of women at each age and SLG who have ever held a job for one, two, or three years; Figures 4.10, 4.11, and 4.12 plot the percentages for the four SLGs for each successive job duration. Like the men, young women in higher SLGs make the transition to stable employment more rapidly. Most notably, women leaving school with a college degree or with some college overtake the less educated groups much more rapidly compared with the men. This difference is due to the speed with which high school dropout and graduate women make the transition compared

Table 4.7

Percentage of Women, by School-Leaving Group and Age, Ever in a Job 1, 2, and 3 Years

Age	N	Duration of Longest Job Ever Held		
		1 Year	2 Years	3 Years
a. High school dropouts				
16	821	0.0	0.0	0.0
17	812	0.8	0.0	0.0
18	803	11.1	0.4	0.0
19	793	24.6	4.6	0.1
20	786	37.2	9.1	2.8
21	782	49.3	13.5	5.1
22	776	55.5	21.3	8.4
23	769	61.3	26.9	14.0
24	760	67.4	32.3	19.6
25	747	71.7	38.3	23.7
26	698	75.2	43.7	26.6
27	500	79.3	48.0	29.9
28	302	82.3	52.6	34.0
b. High school graduates				
16	1307	0.0	0.0	0.0
17	1306	0.0	0.0	0.0
18	1301	0.0	0.0	0.0
19	1290	16.8	0.0	0.0
20	1277	45.3	8.8	0.0
21	1267	63.3	24.0	6.1
22	1253	71.9	37.7	15.9
23	1236	78.1	47.7	25.3
24	1222	82.7	54.1	32.7
25	1198	86.8	60.8	37.4
26	1121	89.5	65.8	44.4
27	877	90.6	69.8	50.0
28	613	92.0	73.5	54.7
29	366	92.2	77.7	58.5
30	171	92.6	80.2	61.2

Table 4.7—continued

Age	N	Duration of Longest Job Ever Held		
		1 Year	2 Years	3 Years
		c. Some college		
16	1005	0.0	0.0	0.0
17	1000	0.0	0.0	0.0
18	999	0.0	0.0	0.0
19	995	0.7	0.0	0.0
20	991	9.7	0.2	0.0
21	986	27.0	3.9	0.2
22	978	45.9	14.4	2.5
23	967	63.1	27.4	9.7
24	955	76.4	40.8	18.4
25	940	84.9	53.0	27.3
26	903	90.0	62.6	36.6
27	783	92.5	70.5	43.1
28	660	93.9	73.5	50.5
29	529	95.2	78.0	54.6
30	365	96.2	81.6	59.1
31	222	96.4	83.5	63.5
		d. College graduates		
16	380	0.0	0.0	0.0
17	378	0.0	0.0	0.0
18	377	0.0	0.0	0.0
19	376	0.0	0.0	0.0
20	374	0.0	0.0	0.0
21	374	0.0	0.0	0.0
22	370	1.6	0.0	0.0
23	367	23.8	1.1	0.0
24	364	70.0	14.4	0.5
25	359	87.1	46.0	10.2
26	348	93.0	65.1	32.2
27	309	95.1	77.1	44.6
28	272	96.8	81.3	52.2
29	236	97.1	84.7	59.8
30	184	97.1	87.9	66.1

NOTES: N is the number of individuals in the sample at least through a given age. Results are shown when sample size for a given age-SLG combination exceeds 150.

with their male counterparts. In fact, regardless of the measure of job duration, women high school graduates make the transition even more slowly than high school dropout men. However, college graduate women and those with some

Figure 4.10—Percentage of Women Ever in a Job 1 or More Years, by Age

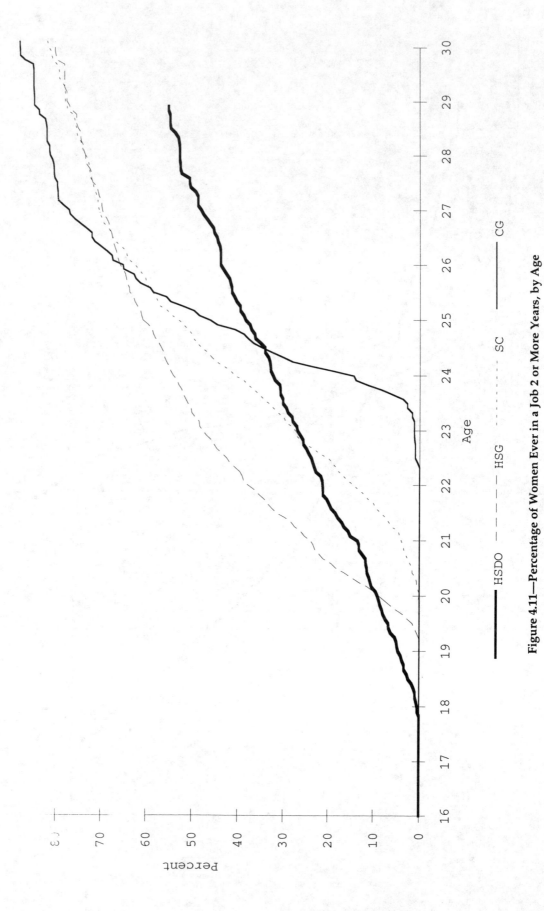

Figure 4.11—Percentage of Women Ever in a Job 2 or More Years, by Age

HSDO ———
HSG – – – –
SC ·········
CG ————

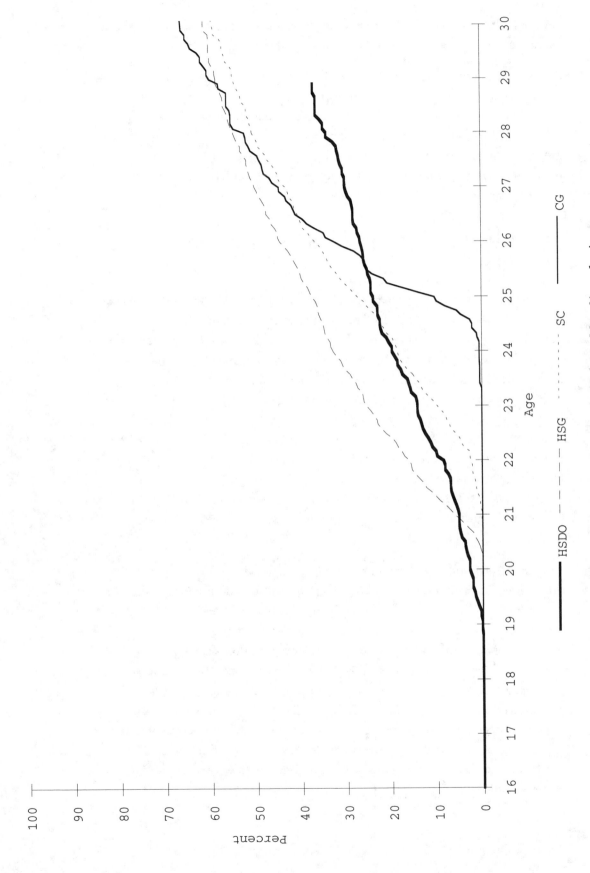

73

Figure 4.12—Percentage of Women Ever in a Job 3 or More Years, by Age

college have patterns that closely mirror those of men in the first few years after leaving school—perhaps because they delay childbearing.

For college graduate women, then, the dynamic process in the early labor market career, whether measured by the number of jobs held or the timing to stable employment, closely matches the experiences of men in the same SLG. At the other end of the spectrum of school leaving, women dropouts and high school graduates face a slower transition to stable employment compared with men, a result that is not reflected in a higher number of jobs held, but in more time spent out of the labor force or looking for work.

The Dynamic Perspective of the School-to-Work Transition

The dynamic analysis presented in this section allows us to examine more closely the complexities of the early labor market experience of young men and women in the NLS-Y. The early career is inherently a dynamic period, with transitions in and out of the labor force, and between jobs of various durations. The employment histories provided in the NLS-Y reveal that this period can be characterized as one in which numerous jobs are held. While young men do not immediately enter jobs that will last for a considerable length of time, such as two or three years, that transition is not delayed until the mid-twenties. The typical, or median, high school graduate who at age 26 (about 8 years after leaving school) has held 6 jobs, has held at least one of those jobs for at least three years. Thus, while he is age 21, three years after leaving high school, the median high school graduate who does not return to school has already entered a job that will last three years.

Of course, the pattern observed for the typical male obscures the extent of the differences that exist between youth who make this transition more rapidly or more slowly. The analysis in this section reveals that the time until a job of one, two, or three years' duration is attained occurs much sooner after leaving school for those who attain more schooling. High school dropouts clearly fare worse in the process, and minority men in this group do even worse. Surprisingly, differences across race/ethnic groups within each SLG for men were less pronounced than the large differences that persist among the SLGs. While women college graduates experience a transition to stable employment that is similar to that of their male counterparts, less educated women make the transition even more slowly than men through more time spent in non-employment.

5. Putting the NLS-Y Sample in Perspective: Trends in Activity Status and Job Tenure

The preceding three sections have analyzed data from the National Longitudinal Survey–Youth. The analysis exploited the continuous employment histories in the NLS-Y to characterize the school-to-work transition in terms of labor market and school enrollment status at a point in time, the number of jobs held, and the age at entering 1-, 2-, and 3-year jobs. No other survey offers this rich level of detail with respect to employment histories.

The drawback of the NLS-Y data is that they refer only to a specific cohort of youth: the NLS-Y sample was drawn from individuals 14 to 21 in late 1978. As we noted in Section 2, our requirement that we observe the initial time of school leaving within the period covered by the continuous employment histories caused us to drop the older respondents. For example, our dropout sample is composed of respondents who were 14 to 17 years old at the time of the first interview; our high school graduate and some college sample includes those aged 14 to 19; our college sample is essentially all of the sampled individuals.

Thus, our results refer primarily to the youth cohort born in the two years before and the two years after 1960. There is considerable interest (and concern) about whether, compared with earlier cohorts, these cohorts have had a harder time making the transition from school to work. Similarly, there are concerns that the transition has become even more difficult since the NLS-Y cohort entered the labor market in the early 1980s. In this section, we try to place the experiences of the NLS-Y cohort of men in the context of earlier and later birth cohorts.

Unfortunately, data comparable to the NLS-Y do not exist for earlier or later cohorts. Instead, we used less comprehensive data from two supplements to the Current Population Survey (CPS). The CPS is a monthly survey of approximately 55,000 households conducted by the Bureau of the Census. The primary purpose of the survey is to provide the official monthly unemployment statistics and other labor market data. For each sampled individual aged 16 and older, the CPS collects basic demographic information (e.g., gender, race/ethnicity, age, educational attainment in years) and detailed information on labor market status for a specific reference week (e.g., labor force status, hours worked, job search efforts). Consistent with the focus in the CPS on measuring

76

labor market status, individuals who do any work are coded as workers, regardless of whether they are enrolled in school.

In addition to the core labor force information, supplemental questions are included on both a regular and an irregular basis. A supplement to the October survey, available annually since 1968, includes detailed information on contemporaneous school attendance for respondents. Combining these supplemental data with the basic CPS information on labor market status, we constructed a time series of static activity status measures similar to those used in Section 3 of this report for young men in various age groups. In addition, in 1973, 1981, 1983, 1987, and 1991, a supplement to the January survey collected information on tenure on the current job. We exploited these data to evaluate changes over time in job tenure for various age groups.

Neither of these CPS data sources permit analyses strictly comparable with those we have conducted using the NLS-Y, our preferred data source. First, the schooling groups we defined using the CPS refer to current educational attainment, not attainment at the time of school leaving (as in our school-leaving groups using the NLS-Y). For example, NLS-Y respondents who were still in college as of the last point at which we observed them (and who have been in school continuously) would not be included in the analyses reported in the preceding sections. In the CPS analysis reported here, they would be included in the some college group. Second, the January CPS measures tenure on the current job. We noted in Section 4 that tenure on the current job provides an overly negative perspective on the transition to stable employment. Nevertheless, examining the time-series patterns in these static and dynamic measures provides useful insights into the likely school-to-work experiences of youth cohorts that entered the labor market between the late 1960s and the early 1990s.

Static Analysis: Activity Status

Since 1968, as part of the October survey, the CPS has included a battery of questions about current school attendance. Combining responses to these questions with responses to the basic labor market information, we constructed static measures of major activity status, assigning individuals hierarchically to the following four mutually exclusive categories: working full time, in school, working part time, and neither working nor in school. These four categories and the hierarchy follow the methodology used for the NLS-Y in Section 3. For example, individuals in school and working full-time (35 or more hours per week) are classified as working full time. Individuals in school and working part time (less than 35 hours per week) are classified as being in school.

Figures 5.1, 5.2, and 5.3 present time trends in these static measures separately for men aged 19 to 21, 23 to 25, and 27 to 29, respectively. Each figure contains four plots showing the percentage of individuals in each of four activity statuses, by year. In each plot (except that for the youngest age group, in which there are few young men who have graduated from college), we show the percentages separately for four education groups: high school dropouts, high school graduates, those with some college, and college graduates.

Across the four educational groups, the patterns reported in the figures show the expected relationships, once we account for the fact that many men in the younger age groups are still in school. In the youngest group (Figure 5.1), for example, most of the some college group are still in school. Thus, the some college group has the highest school attendance rates and the lowest rates in the other three categories. Full-time work, in contrast, is more prevalent among high school graduates compared with high school dropouts. High school dropouts, in turn, are slightly more likely (in most years) to work part time than are high school graduates. Finally, high school dropouts are much more likely than high school graduates to be neither in school nor working.

In the intermediate age group (Figure 5.2), after those progressing continuously through school have completed college, the relative patterns of the schooling groups are even easier to interpret. Those with more education are less likely to be in the residual category (neither working nor in school) and slightly less likely to be working part time. The fact that many of the some college and college graduate groups are still in school (about 20 percent) offsets the strong differentials in the fraction in the residual category. Consequently, there is no clear ordering across the years among schooling groups in the fraction engaged in full-time work.

Finally, turning to the late twenties (Figure 5.3), we can see that school attendance has essentially ended (under 10 percent even in the some college and college graduate groups). Likewise, a very small fraction (less than 10 percent) is classified as working part time, even for high school dropouts for whom part-time work is most common. In most years, well over 90 percent of men aged 27 to 29 are working full time. It is difficult to distinguish the rates for college graduates, some college, and high school graduates. High school dropouts are the exception, because they are less likely to be working full time compared with the other three schooling groups. The pattern is similar, although less pronounced, for the neither working nor in school outcome. Again, high school dropouts are the outlier, with much higher rates in each year compared with more educated men. For the other groups, there is a nearly stable ordering; the fraction in the nonactivity state declines as years of schooling increase.

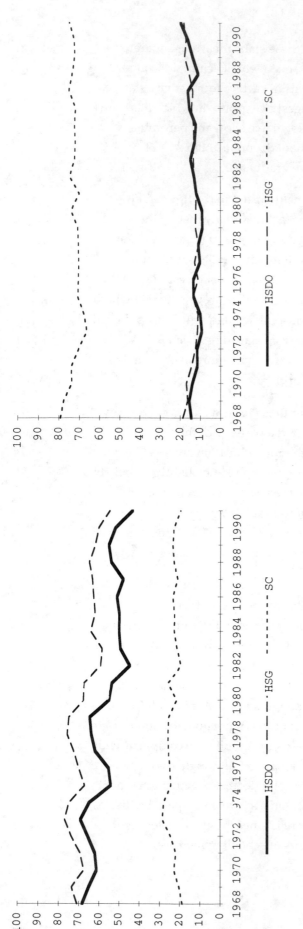

a. Percent working full-time

c. Percent working part-time

HSDO ——— HSG ——— SC

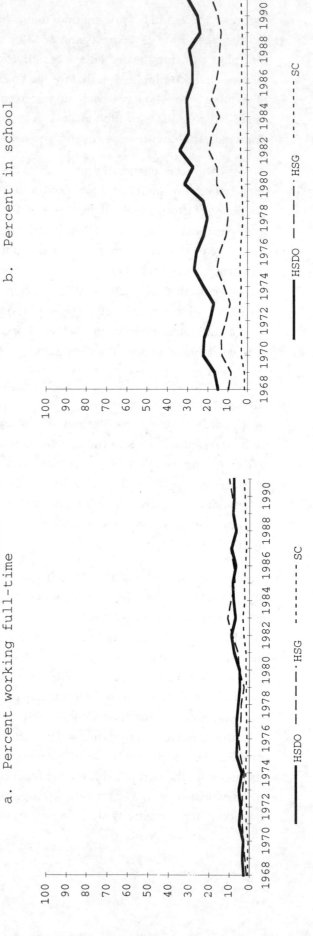

b. Percent in school

d. Percent not working or in school

HSDO ——— HSG ——— SC

Figure 5.1—Primary Activity of Men Aged 19–21, by Schooling Attainment: 1968–1991

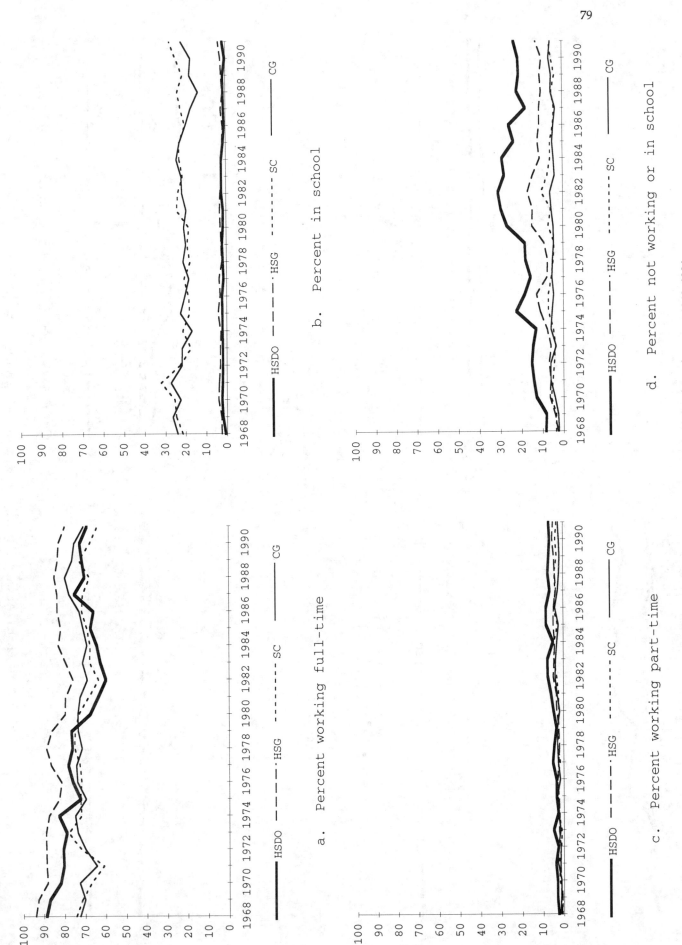

a. Percent working full-time

b. Percent in school

c. Percent working part-time

d. Percent not working or in school

Figure 5.2—Primary Activity of Men Aged 23–25, by School Attainment: 1968–1991

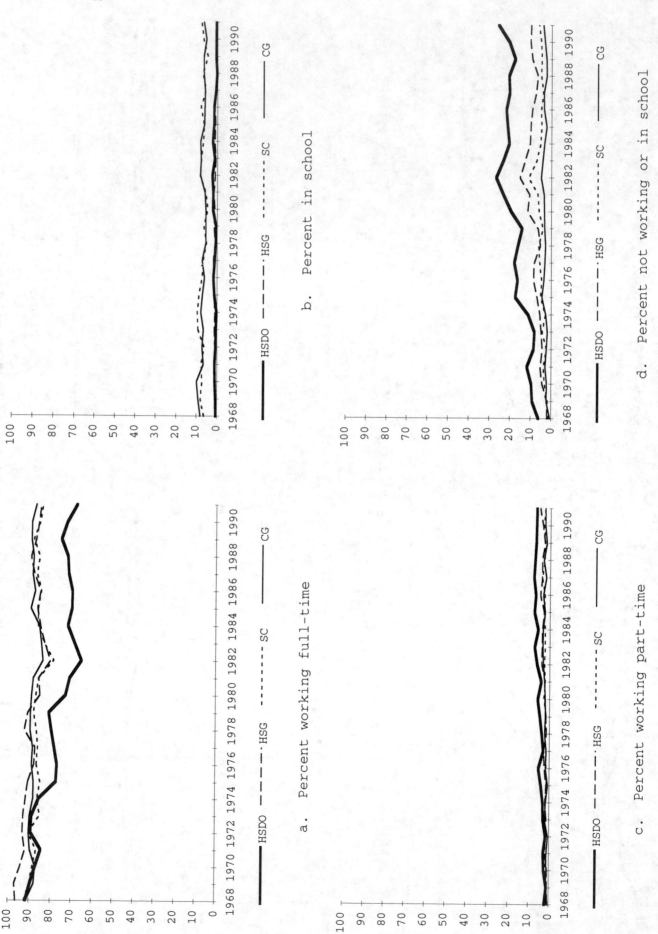

a. Percent working full-time

b. Percent in school

c. Percent working part-time

d. Percent not working or in school

HSDO ----- HSG ------- SC ——— CG

Figure 5.3—Primary Activity of Men Aged 27–29, by Schooling Attainment: 1968–1991

Figures 5.1 through 5.3 also reveal several pronounced changes in the static measure of activity status that occur over this nearly 25-year period. Both absolutely and relative to their peers in higher schooling groups, the situation of high school dropouts has clearly deteriorated. For each of the age groups examined, the fraction engaged in full-time work has fallen approximately 20 to 25 percentage points between 1968 and 1991. For the 23 to 25 year olds, there has actually been a crossover. Through about 1980, dropouts were more likely to be working full time than were those with some college or college graduates. But by the end of the period, they were less likely to be working full time than college graduates and about as likely to be in this category as those with some college.

Almost all the decline in the fraction of high school dropouts engaged in full-time employment has been matched by a corresponding increase in the fraction not engaged in either work or school. There has been little change, in contrast, in the fraction in school or working part time. Among the other education groups there is a small increase (at most a few percentage points) in the fraction neither working nor in school, matched by a decline in the fraction working full time. These modest increases do not come close to the more than 15-percentage-point gain evident for high school dropouts.

Most of the change in activity status for dropouts and the other three schooling groups is concentrated in the period before 1980. While there is considerable cyclical fluctuation thereafter, the trend is less pronounced through the 1980s. For this reason, the school-to-work transition patterns we investigated for the NLS-Y cohort who entered the labor market in the early 1980s are likely to reflect the experiences of later cohorts who entered the labor market throughout the next decade. Conversely, the CPS data also suggest, particularly for high school dropouts, that cohorts of youth who entered the labor market in the late 1960s or the 1970s may have had a better school-to-work transition experience than the NLS-Y cohort.

Moreover, these results are broadly consistent with other trends in the labor market experiences of youths and young adults since 1968. Other authors working with cross-sectional data on employment patterns have found similar patterns, for dropouts, of absolute and relative decreases in full-time employment and increases in not working or not being in school (e.g., Juhn, 1992). The employment patterns evident for this period have been accompanied, as well, by significant changes in the wage structure. Wages for high school dropouts declined both absolutely and relative to those for more educated workers (Klerman and Karoly, 1994).

Dynamic Analysis: Job Tenure

We turn now to more dynamic characterizations of the labor market transitions of young men during the 1970s and the 1980s. Our analysis in Section 4 of this report exploits the longitudinal employment histories of the NLS-Y cohort to identify the age at which young men first entered into jobs that would eventually last 1, 2, and 3 years. Such longitudinal data do not exist for other cohorts. However, in some years (1973, 1981, 1983, 1987, and 1991) the January CPS has included questions concerning tenure in the current job.[1]

At the end of Section 4, we argue that current job tenure is not the ideal statistic for evaluating the extent of the difficulty in the transition to stable employment. Because current job tenure is always less than completed job tenure and because short jobs may be a beneficial aspect of a career involving longer jobs, current job tenure gives too pessimistic a view of the *level* of difficulty in the transition to stable employment. Nevertheless, we must rely on this measure to evaluate the likely changes *over time* in the transition to stable employment. If, as seems reasonable to expect, all three job-tenure measures discussed in Section 4 move together through time, the CPS data allow us to assess variation across youth cohorts in the transition to stable employment.

Figures 5.4, 5.5, and 5.6 present the results from the January CPS. Following the pattern of the earlier figures, results are reported separately for men in three age groups: 19 to 21, 23 to 25, and 27 to 29, respectively. Within each figure, we present four plots showing the percentage of men with 1, 2, 3, and 4 years of tenure on the current job. These percentages are among all men in the age and schooling group, regardless of whether the individual is working (nonworking men are considered to have zero tenure). As above, results are shown separately for the four schooling groups, defined by completed years of schooling as of the interview date. (Figure 5.4 is the exception; college graduates were omitted from it because samples are very small in the 19 to 21 year age group.)

Turning to the figures, consider first the basic patterns by age and schooling groups. Consistent with the results reported for the NLS-Y, at the youngest ages (Figure 5.4), high school graduates are the most likely to have been in a job at least 1 year (about 40 percent). By comparison, the some college and high school dropout groups have similar rates (about 25 to 30 percent). The differential between the three schooling groups narrows as the measure of job tenure lengthens.

---

[1] These data have been used before to analyze various aspects of job tenure: e.g., Hall (1982), Ureta (1992).

a. Percent with 1 or more years of job tenure

——— HSDO — — — HSG ······· SC

b. Percent with 2 or more years of job tenure

——— HSDO — — — HSG ······· SC

c. Percent with 3 or more years of job tenure

——— HSDO — — — HSG ······· SC

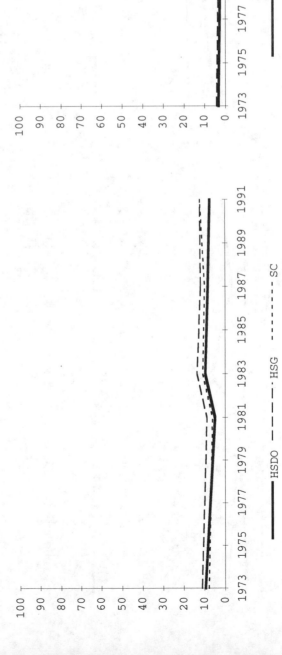

d. Percent with 4 or more years of job tenure

——— HSDO — — — HSG ······· SC

Figure 5.4—Tenure on Current Job for Men Aged 19–21, by Schooling Attainment: 1973, 1981, 1983, 1987, 1991

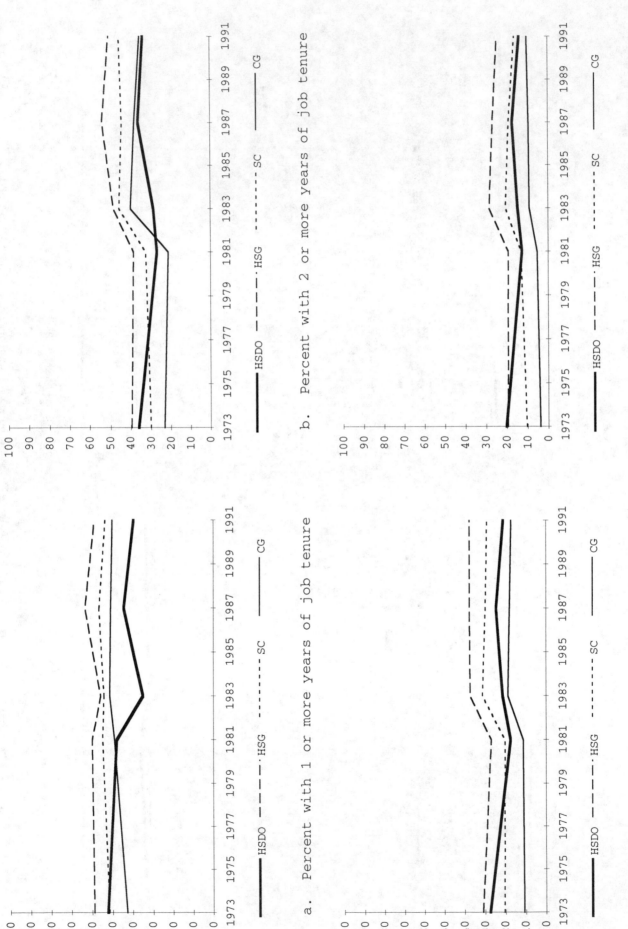

a. Percent with 1 or more years of job tenure

b. Percent with 2 or more years of job tenure

c. Percent with 3 or more years of job tenure

d. Percent with 4 or more years of job tenure

Figure 5.5—Tenure on Current Job for Men Aged 23–25, by Schooling Attainment: 1973, 1981, 1983, 1987, 1991

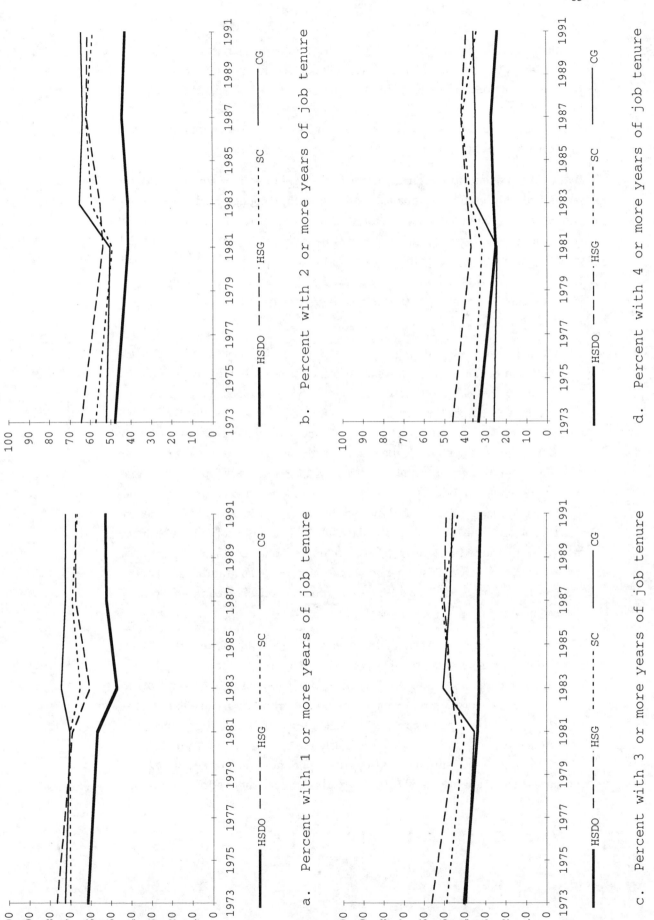

a. Percent with 1 or more years of job tenure

——— HSDO ——— HSG ······· SC ——— CG

b. Percent with 2 or more years of job tenure

——— HSDO ——— HSG ······· SC ——— CG

c. Percent with 3 or more years of job tenure

——— HSDO ——— HSG ······· SC ——— CG

d. Percent with 4 or more years of job tenure

——— HSDO ——— HSG ······· SC ——— CG

Figure 5.6—Tenure on Current Job for Men Aged 27–29, by Schooling Attainment: 1973, 1981, 1983, 1987, 1991

For the middle age group (Figure 5.5), the fraction of those in the some college group with a given level of tenure is typically below the fraction for high school graduates but above the rate for high school dropouts. College graduates lag behind those with less schooling because they typically have entered the labor market at older ages. Even so, college graduates do better even than high school dropouts by the early 1980s for shorter tenures (1 or 2 years).

By the oldest age group (Figure 5.6), the percentage of young men with 1 year of job tenure—high school graduates, some college, and college graduates—looks similar (about 70 percent). Again, the slow start and then convergence of some college and college graduates is probably due to their later entrance into the labor market. Similar orderings are apparent for longer-tenure definitions. For each tenure measure, high school dropouts at these older ages are less likely to have a given level of tenure compared with the other three groups, especially by the early 1980s.

Beyond the age and education group differences, the January CPS data provide time-series information that allows us to judge the representativeness of the NLS-Y cohort that entered the labor market in the early 1980s. Overall, the plots depict relative stability through time in the fraction with a given level of job tenure, although some modest changes did occur over the period covered by the CPS data. For each age group, the fraction with shorter job tenures (1 or 2 years) rose slightly or remained unchanged between 1973 and 1981. During the same period, there was a tendency for the fraction with longer job tenures to decline. The early 1980s, a period marked by back-to-back recessions, led to declines in short-term job tenure (1 year), particularly for high school dropouts in each age group. At the same time, the fraction with longer job tenure (2 to 4 years) increased in the early 1980s, most notably for older college graduates. The changes among 1983, 1987, and 1991 are relatively modest by comparison with the earlier shifts.

With the exception of high school dropouts, at each age the job-tenure rates are similar between 1973 and 1991. Dropouts, by comparison, stand out with an overall decline in the fraction with each measure of job tenure between 1973 and 1991. In almost every figure, a smaller fraction of dropouts are in a job that has lasted 1, 2, 3, or 4 years compared with each of the other schooling groups, a pattern that did not exist in 1973, particularly for those 19 to 21 (Figure 5.3) and 23 to 25 (Figure 5.4). Thus, again, dropouts experienced declines in these measures of job stability both absolutely and relative to more educated young men.

We conclude, as we did from the October CPS data, that results for static and dynamic labor market experiences based on the NLS-Y cohort are likely to closely reflect the experience of both earlier and later cohorts for men who entered the labor market with at least a high school degree. In contrast, high school dropouts who entered the labor market before the NLS-Y cohort probably experienced less difficulty in the transition from school to work; the reverse would be true for more recent labor market entrants.

Discussion

In this section, we have used supplemental data from the October and January CPS to explore the robustness of the school-to-work analysis based on the NLS-Y data. For the three highest schooling groups, the picture that emerges is one of relative stability in the early labor market experience. The fraction of high school graduates, those with some college, and college graduates engaged in work or school between the ages of 19 and 29 changed little during the 1970s and 1980s. Likewise, job-tenure distributions for young men in the mid-1980s (the period covered by the NLS-Y data) look similar to those for the early 1970s and for the early 1990s. Thus, we conclude that our NLS-Y–based characterization of the transition to stable employment is likely to reflect the experiences of earlier and later cohorts of U.S. youth.

The lowest schooling group, high school dropouts, is the exception to this general picture of stability through time. Compared with earlier cohorts, young dropouts today are less likely to be working full time and more likely to be neither working nor in school. At the same time, the job-tenure distribution for these less educated youth appears to have worsened through the 1970s and 1980s; the largest effect is at older ages and longer-tenure points. These results imply that our NLS-Y–based characterization of the transition to stable employment for high school dropouts is probably too pessimistic for the early 1970s and too optimistic for the early 1990s.

88

6. Conclusions

This study has used the National Longitudinal Survey—Youth to reexamine the school-to-work transition among young U.S. men and women in the 1980s. We confirm the results documented in previous research: A large share of young males are neither in school nor working full time after leaving school, especially those who leave school prior to obtaining any post-secondary education. In addition, in the years shortly after leaving school, these young men hold many jobs. Broadly similar patterns hold for women, although their activity status and job-holding patterns are affected by childbearing and childrearing.

From this static analysis of work-history "snapshots," we proceeded to dynamic analyses of the transitions to stable employment. We used a different and, we argue, preferable measure from that used previously. As a result, we find less support for the common perception that the typical high school graduate mills about in the labor market until well into his twenties. By age 19, the typical male high school graduate (measured as the male at the median of the job-duration distribution) has already entered a job that will last at least a year. The corresponding ages for entering jobs that last two or more and three or more years are 20 and 22. For young male high school graduates who do not return to school, the time to reach these job-tenure points occurs a few months to one year earlier. These results suggest that the median high school graduate does not move immediately from school to a long-term job. However, he will enter a long-term job (lasting at least two or three years) in his early twenties—not the mid- or late twenties claimed by some other analysts. Thus, for the median student, the transition to more stable employment does not appear to be a major problem. These longer-tenure jobs may be "dead-end" by some other criteria (absolute earnings, earnings growth), but not by their longevity.

There is, however, considerable diversity with the school-leaving groups we examined. The above characterization holds for the male high school graduate at the middle of the job-duration distribution. This means that half of the men in this school-leaving group achieve stable employment at an even faster pace, and the other half proceeds more slowly. For instance, male high school graduates at the 75th percentile do not reach a 1-, 2-, or 3-year-tenure job until the ages of 20, 23, and 25; those at the 25th percentile attain these milestones two, five, and six years earlier, respectively. For high school dropouts, the time to reach this status is even longer. Among men, blacks and, often, Hispanics within any given school-leaving group also make the transition to stable employment more slowly. These results suggest that while "milling about" is less characteristic of the experience of the typical high school graduate, it is a more accurate description of the early labor market career for most high school dropouts, especially minority men.

We further document that the proportion of young people who could be considered milling about is sensitive to the concept of job duration used. Our concept—ever having held a job lasting M years—presents a more favorable view of the transition than analyses based on whether the current job will last M years, or whether the current job has already lasted M years. Nevertheless, we believe that our concept is the most natural one, because it is based on the experience of *ever* holding a job for a given tenure. We are inclined to believe that whether a current job has lasted or will last that long is of less importance: Job turnover, according to standard search models, follows from the process of trying out different jobs, thereby producing better matches between an individual's skills and the needs of the employer.

The bulk of the analysis is based on school-to-work experiences of the cohort of youth surveyed in the NLS-Y, a group that entered the labor market in the early 1980s. An analysis of data from the Current Population Survey reveals that the experiences of young men in the NLS-Y cohort were similar to the experiences of young men who entered the labor market in the 1970s through the early 1990s. The stability of both static and dynamic measures of early labor market experience based on the CPS is most evident for youth with at least a high school degree.

High school dropouts, by comparison, appear to have faced a more difficult transition into the labor market in the early 1990s than in the late 1960s or early 1970s. Compared with earlier cohorts, young dropouts today are increasingly less likely to be working full time and more likely to be neither working nor in school. At the same time, the job-tenure distribution for these less educated youth appears to have worsened through the 1970s and 1980s; the largest effect is most apparent at older ages and longer-tenure points. These results imply that our NLS-Y–based characterization of the transition to stable employment for high school dropouts is probably too pessimistic for the early 1970s and too optimistic for the early 1990s.

From a policy perspective, these results cast doubt on some of the current school-to-work initiatives. For most high school graduates, stable employment as defined in this analysis is attained relatively quickly (by the early twenties). Thus, programs to encourage the transition to longer-tenure jobs may be based on an erroneous view of the school-to-work transition experience of most (but not all) high school graduates. At the same time, our analysis indicates that youth who leave school before completing a high school degree take considerably more time to achieve longer tenure with a given employer. Finally, these results cast doubt on the suggestion that employers may be reluctant to provide training to young workers because they are concerned that young workers will leave before the firm recovers the cost of training. At least among high school graduates and those who enter the labor market with additional post-secondary schooling, there is evidence of stable employment early in the labor market career.

Appendix

A. Distribution of Sample by School-Leaving Groups

Table A.1 presents the sample distribution separately for men and women, by age at first interview. The total sample was disaggregated by the assigned school-leaving group (SLG), using the method described in Section 2. Table A.1 also shows the fraction of individuals who could not be assigned to an SLG because they left school before January 1978 or because they had missing data.

Table A.1

Weighted Distribution of School-Leaving Groups for Men and Women,
by Age at First Interview (1979)

Age	N	HSDO	HSG	SC	CG	BA+	<78	Missing
				a. Men				
14	504	33.31	35.00	16.62	4.97	1.59	0.00	8.31
15	807	35.32	31.83	17.87	7.02	2.99	0.13	4.84
16	781	33.95	31.39	13.17	7.38	1.57	1.12	11.42
17	753	24.63	33.03	16.05	7.03	1.97	7.73	9.56
18	770	15.46	30.80	12.64	6.37	2.08	22.82	9.93
19	642	3.79	19.16	14.34	6.70	5.19	44.61	6.21
20	620	0.76	2.07	12.89	8.77	2.70	68.12	4.69
21	558	0.00	0.62	9.49	11.12	3.83	70.88	4.06
22	144	0.00	0.00	7.95	4.46	1.34	83.13	3.14
Total	5579	17.78	22.30	13.95	7.35	2.71	28.67	7.24
				b. Women				
14	444	25.25	34.61	20.12	11.04	2.27	0.00	6.71
15	759	27.98	38.39	17.87	6.69	2.44	0.13	6.50
16	783	26.95	37.66	14.31	7.27	2.77	1.37	9.67
17	751	17.29	35.10	20.47	8.34	2.30	6.81	9.69
18	769	9.85	27.23	23.75	8.94	2.75	18.93	8.55
19	755	2.22	14.82	19.20	7.95	2.37	47.48	5.96
20	688	0.62	1.62	19.14	6.75	1.65	65.38	4.84
21	728	0.03	0.00	9.02	8.37	1.24	76.81	4.53
22	150	0.00	0.00	8.13	9.67	4.33	72.44	5.43
Total	5827	12.88	22.52	17.60	8.11	2.28	29.62	6.99

NOTES: <78   School leaving occurred before January 1978 (excluded from sample as missing data).

Missing   Specific missing data problems, in order of importance: unable to distinguish high school diploma from high school equivalency certificate, left school during missing interview, still in school, invalid BA date (excluded from sample as missing data).

B. Sensitivity of Results to an Alternative SLG Definition

In Section 2, we defined five school-leaving groups (SLGs) according to a sample member's work and schooling status. We designated school as the primary activity only if an individual is attending school and not working more than 35 hours per week. Once we observed four to six consecutive months (depending on the time of year) when the individual was no longer engaged in schooling as the primary activity, the individual was assigned an SLG by the highest level of schooling attained up to the point of school departure. As we noted in Section 2, an individual's returning to school meant that the SLG we assigned does not necessarily correspond to the final level of schooling attainment.

In this appendix, we replicate the results presented in the body of the report for men, using a modified definition of SLGs. Since many youth attend school while working full time, our alternative SLG definition considers school the primary activity, even when an individual is working more than 35 hours per week, provided he or she has not yet received a high school diploma or a GED. By this definition, the dropout group is restricted to those who stop attending school altogether for four to six months, without obtaining a high school diploma or GED. According to Table B.1 (which corresponds to Table 2.2), using this alternative SLG definition results in a smaller (reweighted) fraction of the sample being assigned to the dropout category (29.0 percent versus 36.9 percent) and a larger fraction being assigned to each of the remaining SLGs.

Table B.2 and Figure B.1 (corresponding to Table 2.3 and Figure 2.1) show that a smaller fraction of dropouts and high school graduates ever returned to school or returned full time under the alternative SLG definition. Consequently, over half of the individuals classified as dropouts using the alternative definition never attain a GED or diploma, while the fraction is just under 40 percent using the approach described in Section 2. Of the dropouts who return to school, the ratio of GEDs to diplomas is 4 to 1, in contrast to a nearly 1-to-1 ratio obtaining GEDs and diplomas using the original SLG definition. The patterns in return to school are little changed for the other three SLGs. The distribution of final schooling attainment is the same using the two definitions.

The individuals classified as dropouts using the alternative SLG definition are a more "select" group, consisting of those who initially leave school without a high

Table B.1

Size of School-Leaving Groups for NLS-Y Men and Women

SLG	N	Percentage		
		Unweighted	Weighted	Reweighted
		a. Men		
HSDO	1032	18.5	14.4	29.0
HSG	1441	25.8	26.1	39.4
SC	839	15.0	16.2	21.1
CG	337	6.0	8.0	7.4
BA+	130	2.3	3.0	3.1
<78	1318	23.6	24.8	—
Missing	482	8.7	7.6	—
Total	5579	100.0	100.0	100.0
		b. Women		
HSDO	798	13.7	10.2	23.0
HSG	1423	24.4	24.7	41.7
SC	1073	18.4	18.9	22.5
CG	396	6.8	8.5	9.9
BA+	113	1.9	2.4	2.9
<78	1577	27.1	28.0	—
Missing	447	7.7	7.3	—
Total	5827	100.0	100.0	100.0

NOTES: Based on alternative definition of school-leaving groups as described in this appendix. Variance of sum of percentages from 100.0 percent is due to rounding errors.

<78   School leaving occurred before January 1978 (excluded from sample as missing data).

Missing   Specific data problems, in order of importance: unable to distinguish high school diploma from high school equivalency certificate (GED), left school during missing interview, still in school, invalid BA date (excluded from sample as missing data).

Reweighted   Weighted percentages within the observations for which we could assign an SLG among 14–15-year-olds at the first interview (among whom "<78" is very rare).

school degree and who are less likely to ever return to school and receive a diploma. This selectivity is evident in a comparison of the static and dynamic perspectives of the school-to-work transition for dropouts using the two definitions. Table B.3 and Figures B.2 and B.3 (corresponding to Table 3.1 and Figures 3.1 and 3.2) present the static labor force status for men in the four SLGs, by age. Although the patterns are similar for men within the three highest SLGs

Table B.2

**Percentage Distribution of Completed Schooling for NLS-Y Men and Women,
by School-Leaving Groups**

	Total		Returned to school (%)		Final high school degree status (%)			Final post-HS degree status (%)	
SLG	N	Percentage	Ever	Full time	Drop-out	GED	Diploma	BA	MA+
a. Men									
HSDO	1032	27.3	41.1	39.8	51.7	38.7	9.6	1.0	0.0
HSG	1441	38.1	40.0	26.4	0.0	0.0	100.0	4.9	0.2
SC	839	22.2	82.7	59.2	0.0	0.0	100.0	36.5	6.5
CG	337	8.9	60.7	21.8	0.0	0.0	100.0	100.0	14.5
BA+	130	3.4	58.1	32.7	0.0	0.0	100.0	100.0	52.6
Total	3779	100.0			14.1	10.6	75.2	22.6	4.6
b. Women									
HSDO	798	21.0	51.6	50.6	49.0	39.1	11.8	2.0	0.4
HSG	1423	37.4	39.8	28.9	0.0	0.0	100.0	3.9	0.4
SC	1073	28.2	78.1	57.3	0.0	0.0	100.0	31.0	4.1
CG	396	10.4	59.0	26.3	0.0	0.0	100.0	100.0	15.7
BA+	113	3.0	61.4	40.7	0.0	0.0	100.0	100.0	42.7
Total	3803	100.0			10.3	8.2	81.5	24.0	4.3

NOTES: Based on alternative definition of school-leaving groups as described in this appendix. Percentages may not add up to 100.0 because of rounding.

The sample consists of all individuals for whom we could assign an SLG through the last interview they completed (through 1990). *Full-time school* is being in school and working less than 35 hours per week. Final degree attainment is based on the last available interview.

The high school dropout, GED, and diploma columns are mutually exclusive and exhaustive (everyone is either a dropout, has a GED, or has a high school diploma).

regardless of the SLG definition, those classified as dropouts using the alternative definition are more likely to be not working or not in school at each age, and less likely to be engaged in full-time work or in school.

From a dynamic perspective, individuals classified as dropouts using the alternative SLG definition also fared worse in making the transition to stable employment. Table B.4 (corresponding to Table 4.1) reveals that the distribution of the number of jobs held at each age by SLG is nearly unchanged under the alternative SLG definition. However, as seen in Table B.5 and Figures B.4 through B.9 (corresponding to Table 4.4 and Figures 4.1 through 4.6), the transition to stable employment measured by job tenure occurs more slowly for high school dropouts under the alternative SLG definition. Instead of reaching the 1-, 2-, and 3-year-tenure point at ages 20, 23, and 26 under the original

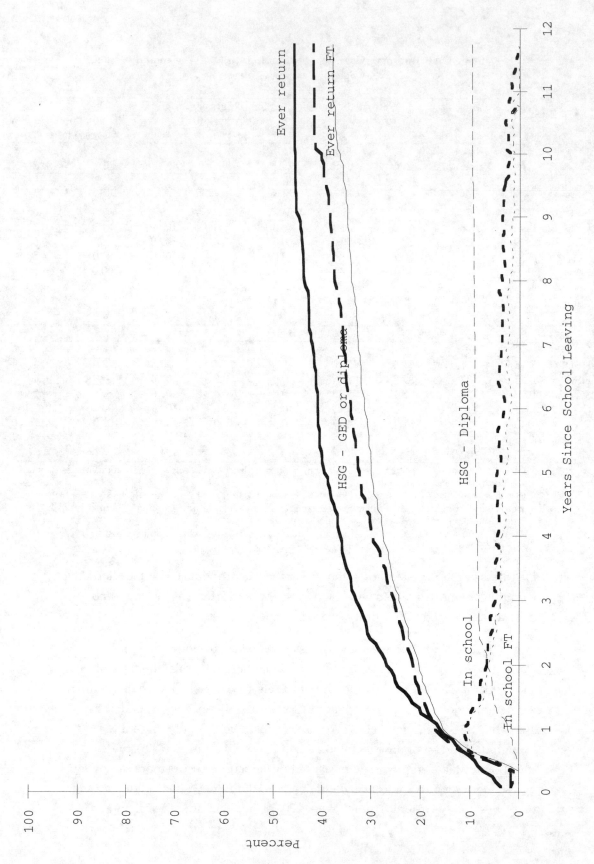

Figure B.1—Return to School and Diploma Receipt for Male High School Dropouts

Table B.3
Static Labor Force Status for Men, by School-Leaving Group and Age

Age	N	Working full time	In school, not working full time	Working part time, not in school	Not working, not in school
			Percentage		
		a. High school dropouts			
17	284	38.0	7.7	16.2	38.1
18	589	47.7	5.3	13.5	33.5
19	818	56.9	4.2	10.6	28.3
20	878	61.4	4.4	7.4	26.8
21	879	65.2	2.9	6.6	25.3
22	868	67.7	2.9	7.9	21.5
23	853	68.4	2.9	6.4	22.3
24	833	69.2	1.9	8.2	20.7
25	815	74.3	1.1	6.2	18.4
26	740	72.3	1.0	6.9	19.9
27	549	74.8	1.0	6.2	18.1
28	353	71.7	2.8	4.6	20.9
29	180	77.6	0.3	2.4	19.6
		b. High school graduates			
18	416	56.8	0.9	23.7	18.6
19	1159	66.7	6.0	13.1	14.2
20	1362	70.1	6.9	11.2	11.8
21	1380	74.7	5.4	8.8	11.1
22	1366	79.1	4.3	6.8	9.9
23	1356	83.0	3.8	5.5	7.7
24	1338	84.7	2.2	6.0	7.1
25	1312	88.4	1.5	4.4	5.7
26	1215	88.1	1.2	4.2	6.4
27	967	89.0	1.8	5.6	3.6
28	725	90.1	0.9	3.6	5.4
29	471	88.9	2.8	3.0	5.3
30	236	88.5	2.1	5.1	4.3

Table B.3—continued

Age	N	Percentage			
		Working full time	In school, not working full time	Working part time, not in school	Not working, not in school
			c. Some college		
19	195	69.3	8.4	12.7	9.6
20	455	64.2	18.3	10.2	7.3
21	624	64.7	22.8	4.6	7.8
22	715	63.8	24.1	7.0	5.1
23	755	67.0	17.5	7.6	7.9
24	775	77.1	10.2	5.5	7.1
25	766	80.5	9.0	6.4	4.0
26	724	83.0	7.4	5.1	4.5
27	594	84.6	5.6	4.4	5.5
28	482	88.2	4.0	4.2	3.7
29	356	86.2	4.4	4.1	5.3
30	247	85.4	4.4	3.7	6.5
31	158	85.8	5.1	2.7	6.3
			d. College graduates		
23	269	80.5	5.3	5.7	8.5
24	309	83.0	6.5	3.3	7.1
25	316	90.6	4.3	2.6	2.6
26	301	87.1	7.1	2.7	3.1
27	261	90.4	3.0	3.8	2.8
28	219	96.1	1.2	1.6	1.2
29	176	94.5	2.1	0.8	2.7

NOTE: Based on alternative definition of school-leaving groups as described in this appendix.

definition, the median dropout reached these points at ages 20, 24, and 28 under the alternative definition. The variance in the distribution is also more substantial for dropouts, using the alternative SLG definition. Under the alternative definition, the results for the other three SLGs are little changed, except that the median high school graduate entered the 3-year-tenure job at age 21 instead of age 22 according to the original definition.

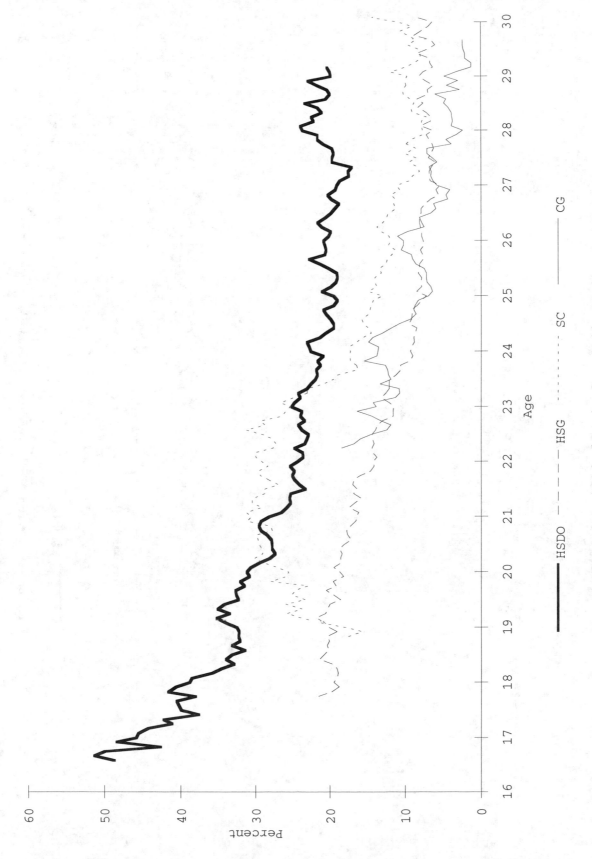

Figure B.2—Percentage of Men in School-Leaving Group Neither Working Nor in School

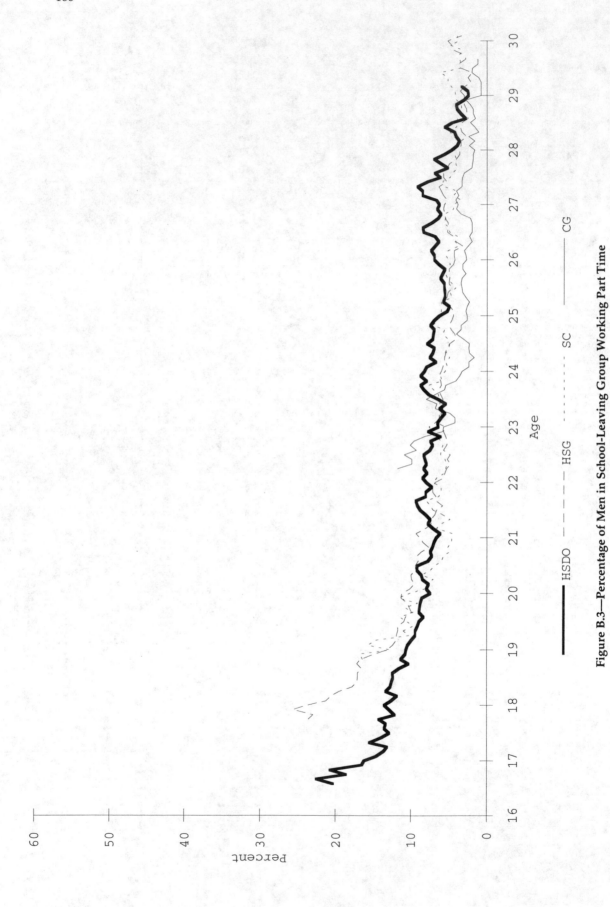

Figure B.3—Percentage of Men in School-Leaving Group Working Part Time

Table B.4

Number of Jobs Held by Men, by School-Leaving Group and Age at Mean, and at 25th, 50th, and 75th Percentiles of Distribution

Age	N				HSDO				HSG				SC				CG			
	HSDO	HSG	SC	CG	Mean	25th	50th	75th	Mean	25th	50th	75th	Mean	25th	50th	75th	Mean	25th	50th	75th
17	934	1431	833	332	0.3	0	0	0	0.0	0	0	0	0.0	0	0	0	0.0	0	0	0
18	920	1421	829	332	1.0	0	1	2	0.3	0	0	1	0.0	0	0	0	0.0	0	0	0
19	905	1407	826	330	2.1	1	2	3	1.4	1	1	2	0.3	0	0	0	0.0	0	0	0
20	893	1397	822	328	3.1	2	3	5	2.4	1	2	3	1.0	0	1	2	0.0	0	0	0
21	885	1382	808	327	3.9	2	3	6	3.1	2	3	4	1.9	1	2	3	0.0	0	0	0
22	873	1369	801	325	4.8	3	5	7	3.8	2	3	5	2.8	1	2	4	0.4	0	0	1
23	856	1359	794	321	5.6	3	5	8	4.5	2	4	6	3.6	2	3	5	1.3	1	1	2
24	837	1338	788	319	6.3	4	6	9	5.1	3	5	7	4.4	2	4	6	1.9	1	2	3
25	819	1315	770	318	7.0	4	7	9	5.6	3	5	8	5.1	3	5	7	2.5	1	2	3
26	744	1216	727	302	7.7	5	7	10	6.1	3	5	8	5.6	3	5	8	2.8	1	2	4
27	551	967	595	261	8.3	5	8	10	6.5	3	6	9	6.2	3	5	8	3.2	1	3	4
28	354	725	482	219	8.4	5	8	10	7.0	4	6	9	6.7	4	6	9	3.5	2	3	4
29	181	471	356	177	8.8	6	9	10	7.4	4	7	10	7.0	4	6	9	3.7	2	3	5
30	—	236	247	—	—	—	—	—	7.5	4	7	10	7.3	4	7	10	—	—	—	—
31	—	—	158	—	—	—	—	—	—	—	—	—	7.7	4	7	10	—	—	—	—

NOTES: Based on alternative definition of school-leaving groups as described in this appendix. A value of 10 indicates 10 or more jobs. N is the number of individuals in the sample at least through a given age. Results are shown when sample size for a given age-SLG combination exceeds 150.

Table B.5

Percentage of Men, by School-Leaving Group and Age, Ever in a Job 1, 2, and 3 Years

		Duration of Longest Job Ever Held		
Age	N	1 Year	2 Years	3 Years
		a. High school dropouts		
16	943	0.0	0.0	0.0
17	934	0.4	0.0	0.0
18	920	6.2	0.0	0.0
19	905	19.4	2.5	0.0
20	893	41.0	8.7	1.0
21	885	57.8	22.7	5.0
22	873	68.8	33.7	15.7
23	856	74.2	41.0	23.1
24	837	79.1	47.6	28.3
25	819	84.1	55.4	34.1
26	744	87.7	61.1	40.8
27	551	89.5	63.8	45.7
28	354	91.7	67.7	49.6
29	181	91.9	69.1	55.3
		b. High school graduates		
16	1433	0.0	0.0	0.0
17	1431	0.0	0.0	0.0
18	1421	0.2	0.0	0.0
19	1407	13.4	0.1	0.0
20	1397	50.4	7.6	0.0
21	1382	71.3	29.6	4.7
22	1369	81.3	44.7	21.0
23	1359	88.3	57.1	31.7
24	1338	92.5	67.7	42.4
25	1315	95.3	74.3	51.9
26	1216	96.5	79.8	58.5
27	967	98.4	85.8	65.1
28	725	98.7	88.2	71.4
29	471	99.1	89.8	76.7
30	236	99.3	92.3	79.7

Table B.5—continued

Age	N	Duration of Longest Job Ever Held		
		1 Year	2 Years	3 Years
		c. Some college		
16	836	0.0	0.0	0.0
17	833	0.0	0.0	0.0
18	829	0.0	0.0	0.0
19	826	0.7	0.0	0.0
20	822	9.2	0.2	0.0
21	808	26.3	5.0	0.2
22	801	42.8	16.6	4.2
23	794	58.1	28.2	11.6
24	788	70.0	39.6	20.0
25	770	81.7	49.4	30.8
26	727	89.9	61.7	38.6
27	595	94.9	71.4	50.7
28	482	97.1	76.5	59.6
29	356	99.1	82.1	64.3
30	247	99.1	87.6	70.7
31	158	99.2	88.1	77.3
		d. College graduates		
16	334	0.0	0.0	0.0
17	332	0.0	0.0	0.0
18	332	0.0	0.0	0.0
19	330	0.0	0.0	0.0
20	328	0.0	0.0	0.0
21	327	0.0	0.0	0.0
22	325	0.2	0.0	0.0
23	321	21.5	0.0	0.0
24	319	62.2	16.3	0.0
25	318	79.5	42.1	14.1
26	302	90.8	61.2	36.7
27	261	95.3	73.1	51.6
28	219	97.6	81.7	60.9
29	177	98.3	84.9	69.2

NOTES: Based on alternative definition of school-leaving groups as described in this appendix.

N is the number of individuals in the sample at least through a given age. Results are shown when sample size for a given age-SLG combination exceeds 150.

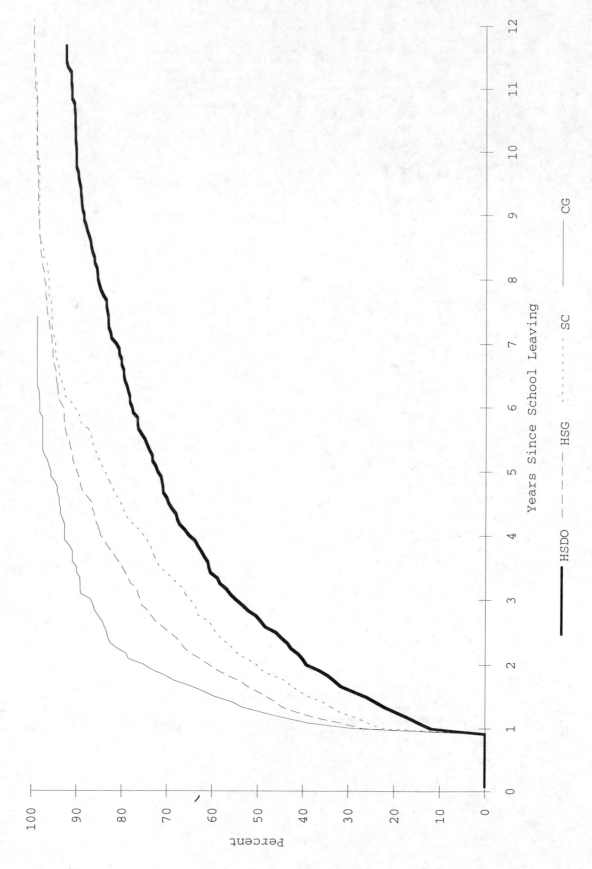

Figure B.4—Percentage of Men Ever in a Job 1 or More Years, by Years Since School Leaving

Figure B.5—Percentage of Men Ever in a Job 2 or More Years, by Years Since School Leaving

Figure B.6—Percentage of Men Ever in a Job 3 or More Years, by Years Since School Leaving

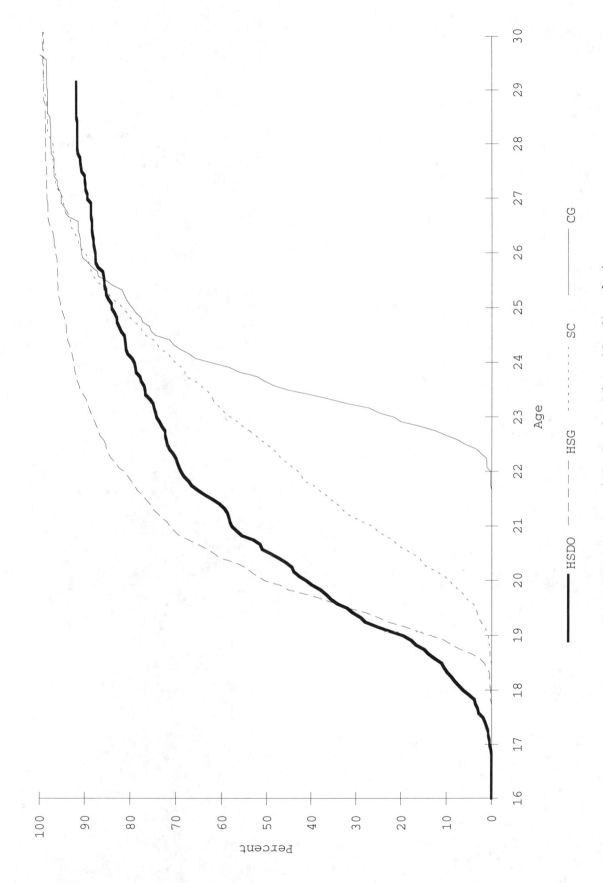

Figure B.7—Percentage of Men Ever in a Job 1 or More Years, by Age

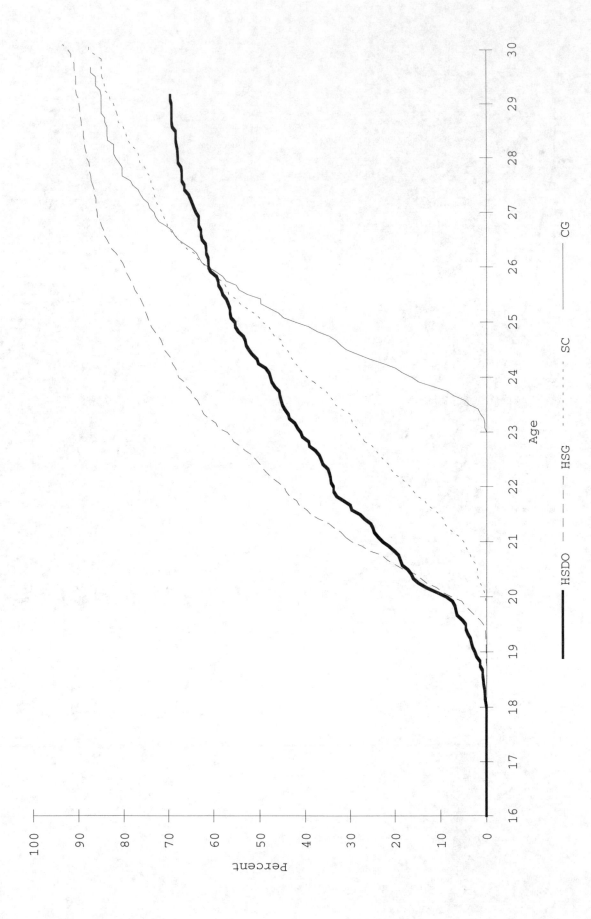

HSDO

HSG

SC

CG

Figure B.8—Percentage of Men Ever in a Job 2 or More Years, by Age

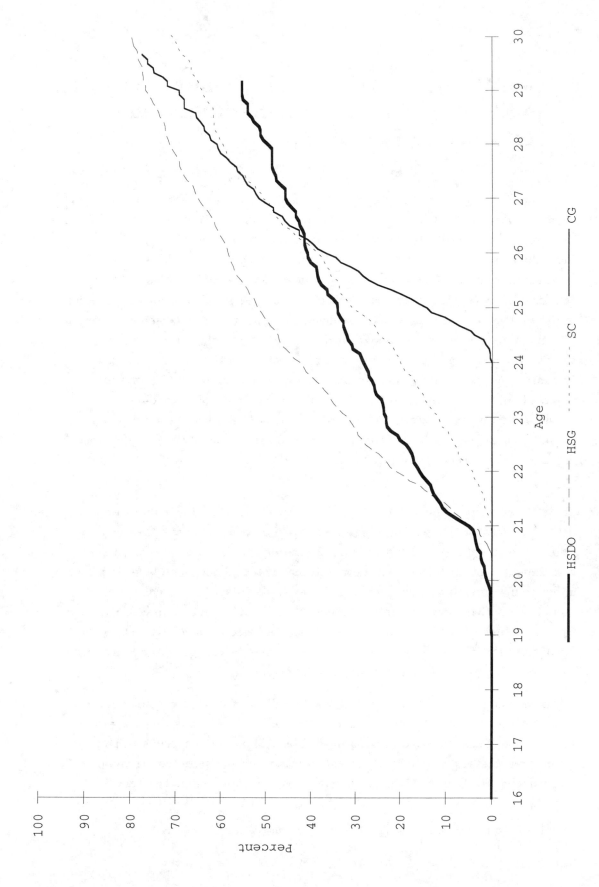

Figure B.9—Percentage of Men Ever in a Job 3 or More Years, by Age

C. Sensitivity of Results of Dynamic Analysis to Stratification, by Whether Individual Returned to School

In this appendix, we reconsider the dynamic analysis of the school-to-work transition for men, stratifying by whether the individual ever returned to school.[1] By the definition of SLG used in the body of the report (and that of Appendix B), an individual who graduates from high school and enters the labor market will be assigned to the high school graduate SLG. If he works for only 6 months and then returns to school for four years to obtain a college degree, he will not enter a 1-year job until about age 23 at the earliest. Consequently, he would be counted among the high school graduate group as one who made the transition to stable employment very slowly. Yet, most observers would consider this pattern to be a success, not a failure. By examining how the transition to stable employment for those who never returned to school differs from that for those who ever returned to school, we avoid the possibility of mixing these two patterns in the early labor market career. In general, the results presented in the body of the report are not substantially altered after we account for the effect of returning to school on the timing of the transition to stable employment.

Table C.1 (corresponding to Table B.4) presents the distribution of the number of jobs held separately for men who never returned to school (panel a) versus those who ever returned to school (panel b). Through age 26, the job distributions are very similar across the two groups. Those who never returned to school hold slightly fewer jobs, although the differences are not striking. For example, by age 26, the average high school dropout who never returned to school has accumulated about three-quarters of a job less than his counterpart who returned to school at some time (7.4 versus 8.1). The largest gap (about 1 job) is evident for those with some college; the gaps are even smaller for those in the high school graduate and college graduate SLGs.

The greater employment "stability" (i.e., fewer jobs held) for those who never return to school is further reflected in the timing of the transition to a job lasting 1, 2, or 3 years. Tables C.2 and C.3 (corresponding to Table B.5) present the results separately for men who never returned to school and for those who ever returned to school, respectively. The timing of the transition is presented graphically in Figures C.1

---

[1]The SLG definition used in this appendix is the same as that defined in Appendix B.

Table C.1

Number of Jobs Held by Men, by School-Leaving Group and Age at Mean, and at 25th, 50th, and 75th Percentiles of Distribution—By Whether Ever Returned to School

a. Never returned to school

Age	N HSDO	N HSG	N SC	N CG	HSDO Mean	HSDO 25th	HSDO 50th	HSDO 75th	HSG Mean	HSG 25th	HSG 50th	HSG 75th	SC Mean	SC 25th	SC 50th	SC 75th	CG Mean	CG 25th	CG 50th	CG 75th
17	579	876	159	133	0.3	0	0	0	0.0	0	0	0	0.0	0	0	0	0.0	0	0	0
18	570	870	156	133	1.0	0	1	2	0.3	0	0	0	0.0	0	0	0	0.0	0	0	0
19	556	866	153	131	2.1	1	2	3	1.3	1	1	2	0.4	0	0	0	0.0	0	0	0
20	548	860	153	130	3.1	2	3	4	2.3	1	2	3	1.1	0	1	2	0.0	0	0	0
21	541	848	148	129	3.9	2	4	6	3.0	2	3	4	1.8	0	2	3	0.0	0	0	0
22	534	838	146	128	4.7	3	5	7	3.6	2	3	5	2.5	1	2	4	0.3	0	0	1
23	520	832	141	125	5.4	3	5	7	4.2	2	4	6	3.1	2	3	4	1.2	1	1	2
24	506	816	141	124	6.1	4	6	8	4.8	3	4	7	3.8	2	3	5	1.8	1	2	3
25	499	804	137	124	6.8	4	7	9	5.4	3	5	7	4.4	2	3	6	2.3	1	2	3
26	454	734	129	113	7.4	4	7	10	5.9	3	5	8	4.9	3	4	6	2.5	1	2	3
27	339	580	—	—	7.9	5	8	10	6.3	3	5	9	—	—	—	—	—	—	—	—
28	220	445	—	—	8.0	5	8	10	6.8	3	6	9	—	—	—	—	—	—	—	—
29	117	299	—	—	8.5	6	8	10	7.1	4	6	9	—	—	—	—	—	—	—	—
30	—	154	—	—	—	—	—	—	7.7	4	6	10	—	—	—	—	—	—	—	—
31	—	—	—	—	—	—	—	—	—	—	—	—	—	—	—	—	—	—	—	—

Table C.1—continued

b. Ever returned to school

Age	N				HSDO				HSG				SC				CG			
	HSDO	HSG	SC	CG	Mean	25th	50th	75th	Mean	25th	50th	75th	Mean	25th	50th	75th	Mean	25th	50th	75th
17	352	555	673	199	0.3	0	0	0	0.0	0	0	0	0.0	0	0	0	0.0	0	0	0
18	347	551	672	199	1.0	0	1	2	0.4	0	0	1	0.0	0	0	0	0.0	0	0	0
19	346	541	672	199	2.2	1	2	3	1.6	1	1	2	0.3	0	0	0	0.0	0	0	0
20	342	537	668	198	3.2	2	3	5	2.5	1	2	3	1.0	0	1	2	0.0	0	0	0
21	341	534	659	198	4.0	2	3	6	3.4	2	3	5	1.9	1	2	3	0.0	0	0	0
22	336	531	654	197	5.0	2	5	7	4.1	2	4	5	2.8	1	3	4	0.4	0	0	1
23	333	527	652	196	5.8	3	5	8	4.8	3	5	6	3.7	2	3	5	1.4	1	1	2
24	328	522	646	195	6.6	3	6	9	5.4	3	5	7	4.5	2	4	6	2.0	1	2	3
25	317	511	632	194	7.4	4	7	10	6.0	3	6	8	5.2	3	5	7	2.6	1	2	4
26	288	482	597	189	8.1	4	7	10	6.5	4	6	9	5.8	3	5	8	3.0	1	3	4
27	210	387	498	167	8.9	5	8	10	6.8	4	7	9	6.3	4	6	8	3.3	2	3	5
28	132	280	406	137	9.1	5	8	10	7.4	4	7	10	6.8	4	6	9	3.7	2	3	5
29	—	172	301	115	—	—	—	—	7.8	5	7	10	7.2	4	6	9	3.7	2	3	6
30	—	—	209	—	—	—	—	—	—	—	—	—	7.5	4	7	10	—	—	—	—
31	—	—	138	—	—	—	—	—	—	—	—	—	7.9	5	7	10	—	—	—	—

NOTES: Based on alternative definition of school-leaving groups as described in Appendix B. A value of 10 indicates 10 or more jobs. N is the number of individuals in the sample at least through a given age. Results are shown when sample size for a given age-SLG combination exceeds 100.

through C.6 (corresponding to Figures B.4 through B.9), where figures a and b plot the results for those who never returned to school and those who ever returned to school, respectively.

Not surprisingly, measured by time since school leaving (Figures C.1 through C.3), those who never returned to school reach the 1-, 2-, and 3-year-tenure points slightly faster than their counterparts who returned to school, although there is some evidence that those who returned to school eventually (within 10 or more years since the time of original school leaving) overtake their peers who never went back to school. Of the four SLGs, the difference is most striking for those with some college.

When age is the point of reference (Figures C.4 through C.6 and Table C.2), dropouts, high school graduates, and college graduates show very similar trajectories regardless of whether they returned to school. Among dropouts, those who never returned to school reach the 1-year-tenure point slightly faster than those who ever returned to school, whereas the differences for the 2-year and 3-year job are very small. In fact, for all three tenure points, the median dropout enters the job at the same age regardless of whether he returned to school. The differences for high school graduates and college graduates are equally small. There is some evidence in Figures C.4 through C.6 that the time until nearly all in the college graduate SLG reach the 1-year-tenure point occurs more rapidly for those who never returned to school, although this is to be expected. The data become almost too sparse, however, to draw firm conclusions.

The some college SLG stands out, with the sharpest contrast between the timing to stable employment by whether the individual returns to school, although the differences are still modest. For those who attended college but left without obtaining a degree and never returned, the transition to stable employment occurred somewhat more quickly. The median male who never returned to school entered the 1-, 2-, and 3-year-tenure jobs at ages 20, 21, and 23, respectively. These points are not reached by the median male who returned to school until one to two years later (ages 21, 23, and 24, respectively). Those who returned to school eventually caught up: By the late twenties, a similar fraction has reached the 1-, 2-, and 3-year-tenure points.

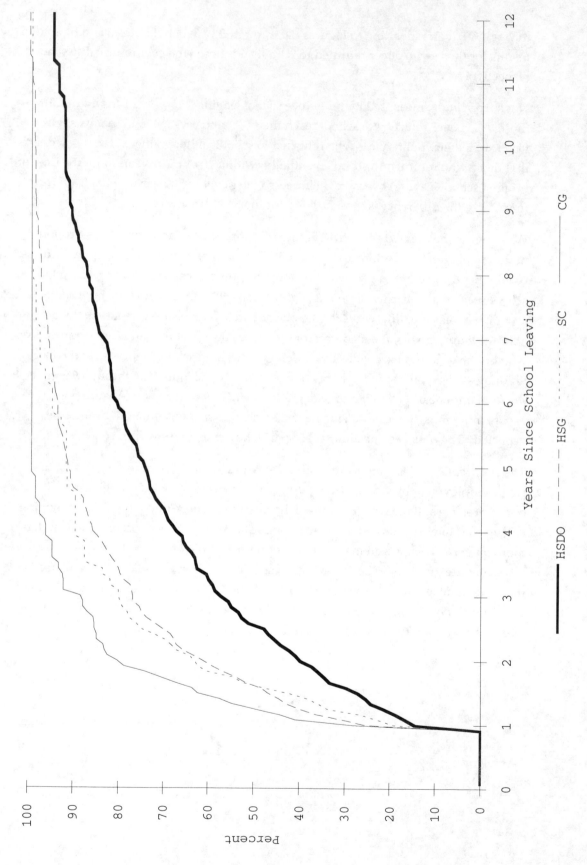

Figure C.1a—Percentage of Men Ever in a Job 1 or More Years, by Years Since School Leaving—Never Returned

Figure C.1b—Percentage of Men Ever in a Job 1 or More Years, by Years Since School Leaving—Ever Returned

116

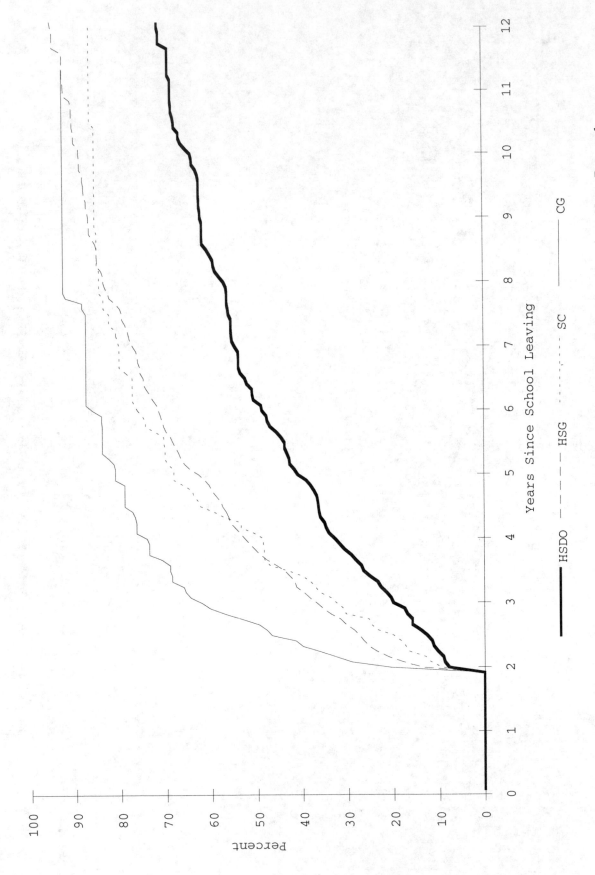

Figure C.2a—Percentage of Men Ever in a Job 2 or More Years, by Years Since School Leaving—Never Returned

117

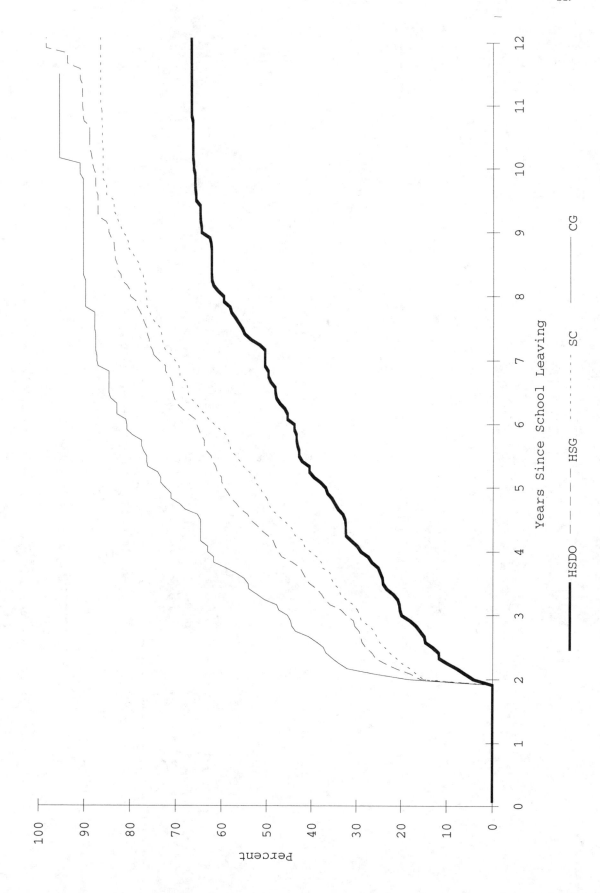

Figure C.2b—Percentage of Men Ever in a Job 2 or More Years, by Years Since School Leaving—Ever Returned

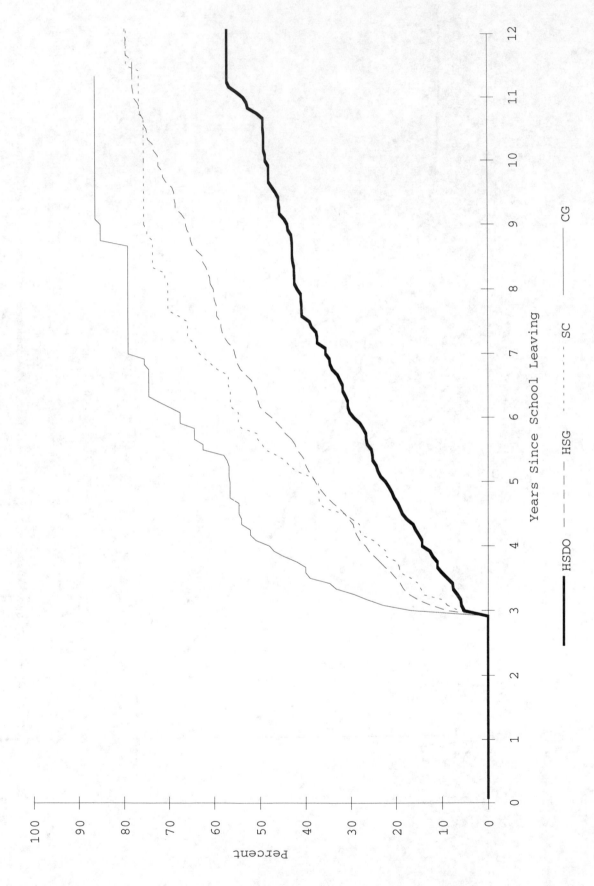

Figure C.3a—Percentage of Men Ever in a Job 3 or More Years, by Years Since School Leaving

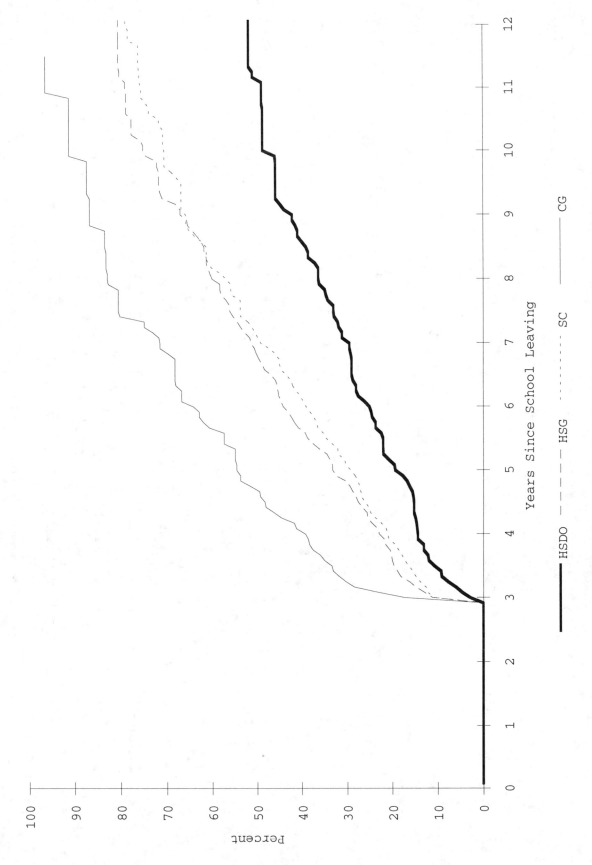

Figure C.3b—Percentage of Men Ever in a Job 3 or More Years, by Years Since School Leaving—Ever Returned

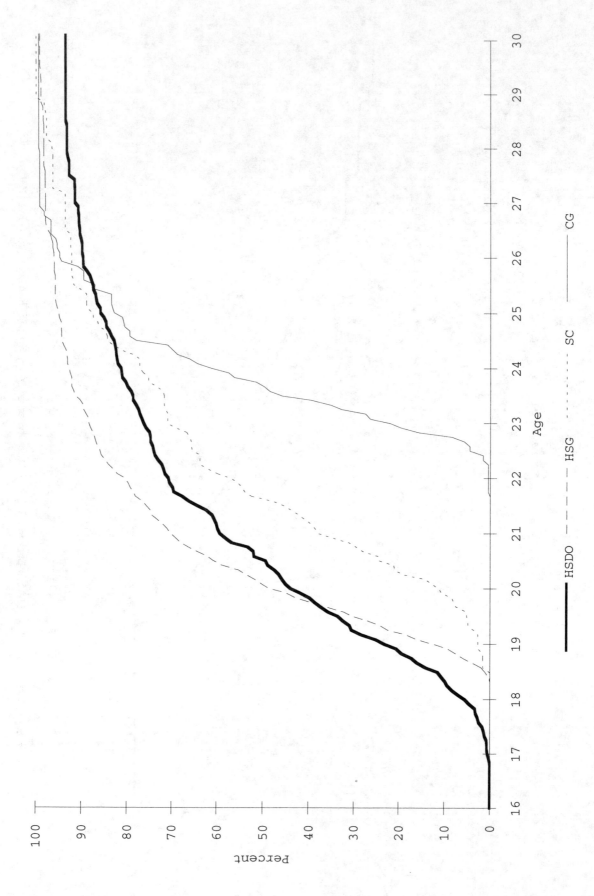

Figure C.4a—Percentage of Men Ever in a Job 1 or More Years, by Age—Never Returned

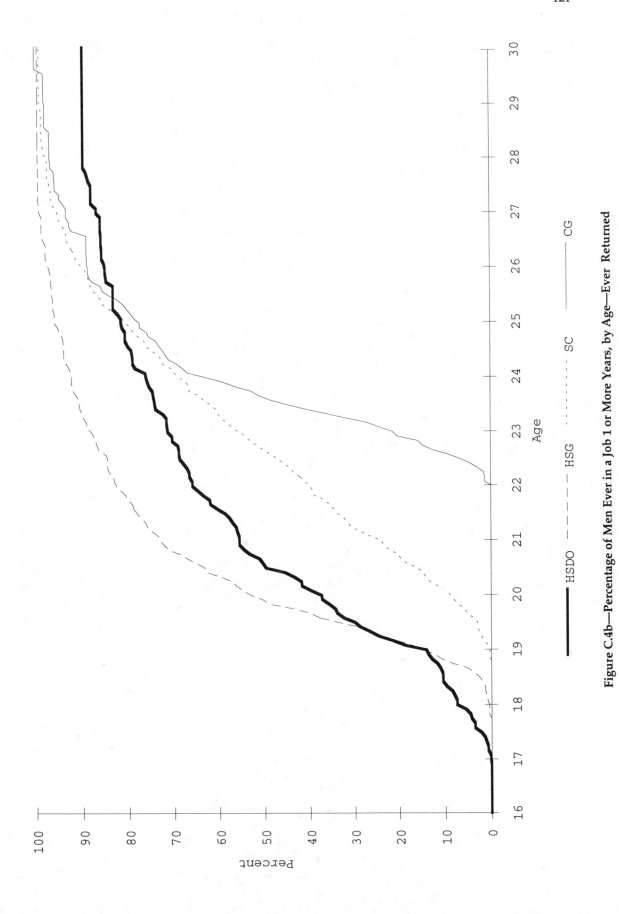

Figure C.4b—Percentage of Men Ever in a Job 1 or More Years, by Age—Ever Returned

Figure C.5a—Percentage of Men Ever in a Job 2 or More Years, by Age—Never Returned

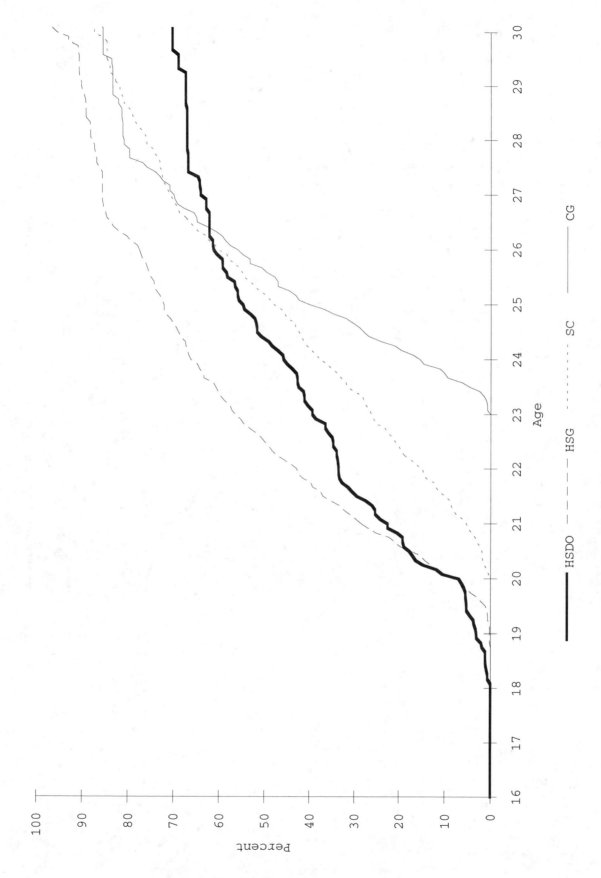

HSDO ——— HSG – – – SC ······· CG ——

Age

Figure C.5b—Percentage of Men Ever in a Job 2 or More Years, by Age—Ever Returned

Figure C.6a—Percentage of Men Ever in a Job 3 or More Years, by Age—Never Returned

Figure C.6b—Percentage of Men Ever in a Job 3 or More Years, by Age—Ever Returned

Table C.2

**Percentage of Men, by School-Leaving Group and Age, Ever in a
Job 1, 2, and 3 Years—Never Returned to School**

Age	N	Duration of Longest Job Ever Held		
		1 Year	2 Years	3 Years
a. High school dropouts				
16	584	0.0	0.0	0.0
17	579	0.5	0.0	0.0
18	570	5.4	0.0	0.0
19	556	23.1	2.1	0.1
20	548	43.9	10.0	0.7
21	541	59.3	23.1	5.6
22	534	70.7	34.1	15.7
23	520	76.3	42.5	23.2
24	506	81.3	49.3	29.7
25	499	85.9	56.3	35.9
26	454	89.7	60.6	42.4
27	339	91.4	63.2	47.4
28	220	93.2	68.1	50.2
29	117	93.5	70.4	57.5
b. High school graduates				
16	877	0.0	0.0	0.0
17	876	0.0	0.0	0.0
18	870	0.0	0.0	0.0
19	866	12.5	0.0	0.0
20	860	48.6	7.2	0.0
21	848	70.3	30.3	4.2
22	838	80.6	46.0	21.9
23	832	88.5	57.4	33.4
24	816	92.7	68.6	42.6
25	804	95.0	75.6	52.8
26	734	96.1	81.2	58.7
27	580	97.9	85.9	65.1
28	445	98.3	88.2	69.6
29	299	98.9	89.5	74.6
30	154	99.2	90.9	78.9

Table C.2—continued

Age	N	Duration of Longest Job Ever Held		
		1 Year	2 Years	3 Years
c. Some college				
16	160	0.0	0.0	0.0
17	159	0.0	0.0	0.0
18	156	0.0	0.0	0.0
19	153	2.6	0.0	0.0
20	153	11.1	1.3	0.0
21	148	37.9	3.6	1.3
22	146	57.1	24.8	3.6
23	141	70.9	38.3	16.0
24	141	77.2	50.4	28.9
25	137	87.5	57.1	41.9
26	129	92.2	68.7	47.0
d. College graduates				
16	135	0.0	0.0	0.0
17	133	0.0	0.0	0.0
18	133	0.0	0.0	0.0
19	131	0.0	0.0	0.0
20	130	0.0	0.0	0.0
21	129	0.0	0.0	0.0
22	128	0.4	0.0	0.0
23	125	22.0	0.0	0.0
24	124	61.3	17.9	0.0
25	124	82.8	45.8	13.1
26	113	94.8	69.8	37.9

NOTES: Based on alternative definition of school-leaving groups as described in Appendix B.

N is the number of individuals in the sample at least through a given age. Results are shown when sample size for a given age-SLG combination exceeds 100.

Table C.3

**Percentage of Men, by School-Leaving Group and Age, Ever in a
Job 1, 2, and 3 Years—Ever Returned to School**

| Age | N | Duration of Longest Job Ever Held | | |
		1 Year	2 Years	3 Years
		a. High school dropouts		
16	356	0.0	0.0	0.0
17	352	0.1	0.0	0.0
18	347	7.4	0.0	0.0
19	346	14.1	3.1	1.4
20	342	37.3	6.9	4.1
21	341	55.5	22.5	15.8
22	336	65.9	33.5	23.1
23	333	71.2	39.4	26.7
24	328	76.0	45.8	31.8
25	317	81.4	54.8	39.0
26	288	84.9	61.3	43.8
27	210	86.7	64.2	49.5
28	132	89.5	67.1	53.4
		b. High school graduates		
16	556	0.0	0.0	0.0
17	555	0.0	0.0	0.0
18	551	0.5	0.0	0.0
19	541	14.9	0.2	0.0
20	537	53.0	8.2	0.1
21	534	72.8	28.5	5.5
22	531	82.5	42.8	19.7
23	527	88.0	56.6	29.0
24	522	92.2	66.3	42.1
25	511	95.8	72.2	50.5
26	482	97.0	77.6	58.2
27	387	99.0	85.8	65.0
28	280	99.3	88.1	74.0
29	172	99.3	90.3	79.7

Table C.3—continued

Age	N	Duration of Longest Job Ever Held		
		1 Year	2 Years	3 Years
		c. Some college		
16	675	0.0	0.0	0.0
17	673	0.0	0.0	0.0
18	672	0.0	0.0	0.0
19	672	0.4	0.0	0.0
20	668	8.8	0.0	0.0
21	659	24.0	5.3	0.0
22	654	40.0	14.9	4.3
23	652	55.6	26.2	10.8
24	646	68.6	37.6	18.3
25	632	80.5	48.0	28.7
26	597	89.5	60.4	37.0
27	498	95.1	70.8	49.0
28	406	97.3	76.1	58.5
29	301	98.9	81.9	63.5
30	209	98.9	87.5	70.1
31	138	99.0	88.1	76.3
		d. College graduates		
16	199	0.0	0.0	0.0
17	199	0.0	0.0	0.0
18	199	0.0	0.0	0.0
19	199	0.0	0.0	0.0
20	198	0.0	0.0	0.0
21	198	0.0	0.0	0.0
22	197	0.0	0.0	0.0
23	196	21.3	0.0	0.0
24	195	62.7	15.4	0.0
25	194	77.5	40.0	14.7
26	189	88.6	56.0	35.9
27	167	93.3	70.0	50.0
28	137	96.7	81.0	59.1
29	115	97.8	83.5	68.9

NOTES: Based on alternative definition of school-leaving groups as described in Appendix B.

N is the number of individuals in the sample at least through a given age. Results are shown when sample size for a given age-SLG combination exceeds 100.

Bibliography

Abraham, Katharine G., and Henry S. Farber. 1987. "Job Duration, Seniority, and Earnings," *American Economic Review*, LXXVII: 279–297.

Altonji, J., and J. Shakoko. 1987. "Do Wages Rise with Job Seniority?" *Review of Economic Studies*, LIV: 437–460.

Becker, Gary S. 1964. *Human Capital: A Theoretical and Empirical Analysis, with Special Reference to Education.* New York: Columbia University Press (for National Bureau of Economic Research [NBER]).

Becketti, Sean, William Gould, Lee Lillard, and Finis Welch. 1988. "The Panel Study of Income Dynamics After Fourteen Years: An Evaluation." *Journal of Labor Economics*, 6 (4, October): 472–492.

Berryman, Sue E., and Thomas Bailey. 1992. *The Double Helix of Education and the Economy.* New York: Columbia University, Teachers College, The Institute on Education and the Economy.

Bowers, Norman. 1980. "Probing the Issues of Unemployment Duration." *Monthly Labor Review*, July: 23–32.

Burdett, K. 1978. "A Theory of Employee Job Search and Quit Rates." *American Economic Review*, LXVIII(1): 212–220.

Bureau of Labor Statistics (BLS). 1992. *Work and Family: Jobs Held and Weeks Worked by Young Adults.* Washington, D.C., Report 827 (August).

Bureau of Labor Statistics. 1993. *Work and Family: Turning Thirty: Job Mobility and Labor Market Attachment.* Washington, D.C., Report 862 (December).

Cameron, Stephen V., and James J. Heckman. 1993. "The Nonequivalence of High School Equivalents." *Journal of Labor Economics*, 11 (January, Part 1): 1–47.

Carrington, William J. 1993. "Wage Losses for Displaced Workers: Is It Really the Firm that Matters?" *Journal of Human Resources*, 28(3): 435–462.

Center for Human Resource Research. 1988. *NLS Handbook.* Columbus: Ohio State University.

Commission on the Skills of the American Workforce (CSAW). 1990. *America's Choice: High Skills or Low Wages*. Rochester, N.Y.: National Center on Education and the Economy.

Doeringer, Peter B., and Michael J. Piore. 1971. *Internal Labor Markets and Manpower Analysis*. Lexington, Mass.: Heath.

Flinn, Christopher J. 1986. "Wages and Job Mobility of Young Workers." *Journal of Political Economy*, 94 (3, Part 2): S88–S110.

Frase, Mary J. 1989. *Dropout Rates in the United States: 1988*. Washington, D.C.: National Center for Education Statistics, U.S. Department of Education, Report 89-609.

Freeman, Richard B., and David A. Wise. 1982. *The Youth Labor Market Problem: Its Nature, Causes, and Consequences*. Chicago: University of Chicago Press.

General Accounting Office. 1991. *Transition from School to Work: Linking Education and Worksite Training*. Washington, D.C., GAO Report HRD-91-105.

Haggstrom, Gus, Thomas J. Blaschke, and Richard J. Shavelson. 1991. *After High School, Then What? A Look at the Postsecondary Sorting-Out Process for American Youth*. Santa Monica, Calif.: RAND, R-4008-FMP.

Hall, Robert E. 1982. "The Importance of Lifetime Jobs in the U.S. Economy." *American Economic Review*, LXXII: 716–724.

Hamilton, S. F. 1990. *Apprenticeship for Adulthood*. New York: Free Press.

Horvath, Francis W. 1982. "Job Tenure of Workers in January 1981." *Monthly Labor Review*, September: 34–36.

Jacobson, Louis S., Robert J. LaLonde, and Daniel G. Sullivan. 1993. "Earnings Losses of Displaced Workers." *American Economic Review*, 83(4, September): 685–709.

Johnson, William R. 1978. "A Theory of Job Shopping." *Quarterly Journal of Economics*, 92 (May): 261–278.

Jovanovic, Boyan. 1979. "Firm-specific Capital and Turnover." *Journal of Political Economy*, 87 (December) : 1246–1260.

Juhn, Chinhui. 1992. "Decline of Male Labor Market Participation: The Role of Declining Market Opportunities." *The Quarterly Journal of Economics*, 107(1): 79–121.

Klerman, Jacob Alex. 1991, 1992. "Pitfalls of Panel Data: The Case of the SIPP Health Insurance Data," in *Proceedings, The 1990's: A Decade of Decisions for Vital and Health Statistics*, Public Health Conference on Records and Statistics, pp. 36–39 (also RAND RP-111).

Klerman, Jacob Alex, and Lynn A. Karoly. 1994. "Trends and Future Directions in Youth Labor Markets: Implications for Army Recruiting," in Mark J. Eitelberg and Stephen L. Mehay, eds., *Marching Toward the 21st Century: Military Manpower and Recruiting*. Westport, Conn.: Greenwood Press, pp. 41–65 (also RAND RP-310).

Lynch, Lisa M. 1993. "The Economics of Youth Training in the United States." *The Economic Journal*, 1292–1302.

Manski, Charles F., and David A. Wise. 1983. *College Choice in America*. Cambridge, Mass.: Harvard University Press.

Mare, Robert D., and Christopher Winship. 1986. "School Enrollment, Military Enlistment, and the Transition to Work: Implications for the Age Pattern of Employment," in *The Transition to Work or Postsecondary Education*. Lexington, Mass.: Lexington Books, pp. 364–495.

Mattilla, J. Peter. 1974. "Job Quitting and Frictional Unemployment." *Amercian Economic Review*, 64(2, March), 235–239.

McCall, Brian P. 1990. "Occupational Matching: A Test of Sorts." *Journal of Political Economy*, 98(1): 45–69.

Meyer, Robert H., and David A. Wise. 1982. "High School Preparation and Early Labor Force Experience," in R. B. Freeman and D. A. Wise, eds., *The Youth Labor Market Problem: Its Nature, Causes, and Consequences*. Chicago: University of Chicago Press.

Michael, Robert T., and Nancy Brandon Tuma. 1984. "Youth Employment: Does Life Begin at 16?" *Journal of Labor Economics*, 2(4): 464–476.

Mincer, Jacob, and Boyan Jovanovic. 1981. "Labor Mobility and Wages," in S. Rosen, ed., *Studies in Labor Markets*. Chicago: University of Chicago Press for NBER, pp. 21–64.

Mincer, Jacob, and Solomon Polachek. 1974. "Family Investments in Human Capital: Earnings of Women." *Journal of Political Economy*, 82(2, Part 2, March/April): S76–S108.

Nolfi, George J., Winship C. Fuller, Arthur J. Corazzini, William H. Epstein, Richard B. Freeman, Charles F. Manski, Valerie I. Nelson, and David A. Wise. 1986. "Experiences of Recent High School Graduates," in *The Transition to Work or Postsecondary Education*. Lexington, Mass.: Lexington Books.

Osterman, Paul. 1980. *Getting Started: The Youth Labor Market*. Cambridge, Mass.: MIT Press.

Osterman, Paul, and Maria Iannozzi. 1993. "Youth Apprenticeships and School-to-Work Transitions: Current Knowledge and Legislative Strategy." Philadelphia, Penn.: National Center on the Educational Quality of the Workforce, Working Paper 14.

Parsons, D. 1991. "The Job Search Behavior of Employed Youth." *Review of Economics and Statistics*, 73(4): 597–604.

Prewo, Wilfred. 1993. "The Sorcery of Apprenticeship." *The Wall Street Journal,* February 12.

Rees, Albert. 1986. "An Essay on Youth Joblessness." *The Journal of Economic Literature,* XXIV(2): 613–628.

Rosenbaum, James E., and Takehiko Kariya. 1989. "From High School to Work: Market and Institutional Mechanisms in Japan." *American Journal of Sociology,* 94(6): 1334–1365.

Rosenbaum, James E., Takehiko Kariya, Rick Settersten, and Tony Maier. 1990. "Market and Network Theories of the Transition from High School to Work: Their Application to Industrial Societies." *Annual Review of Sociology,* 16: 263–299.

Sandell, Steven H., and David Shapiro. 1980. "Work Expectation, Human Capital Accumulation, and Wages of Young Women." *Journal of Human Resources,* 15(Summer): 335–353.

Sicherman, Nachum, and Oded Galor. 1990. "A Theory of Career Mobility." *Journal of Political Economy,* 98(1): 169–192.

Slichter, Sumner. 1919. *The Turnover of Factory Labor.* New York: D. Appleton.

Topel, Robert H. 1991. "Specific Capital, Mobility, and Wages: Wages Rise with Job Seniority." *Journal of Political Economy,* 99 (1): 145–176.

Topel, Robert H., and Michael P. Ward. 1992. "Job Mobility and the Careers of Young Men." *Quarterly Journal of Economics.*

Ureta, Manuelita. 1992. "The Importance of Lifetime Jobs in the U.S. Economy, Revised," *American Economic Review,* 82(1): 322–335.

Veum, Jonathan R., and Andrea B. Weiss. 1993. "Education and the Work Histories of Young Adults." *Monthly Labor Review,* 116(4): 11–20.

Wachter, Michael, and Choongsoo Kim. 1982. "Time Series Changes in Youth Joblessness," in Richard B. Freeman and David A. Wise, eds., *The Youth Labor Market Problem: Its Nature, Causes, and Consequences.* Chicago: University of Chicago Press, pp. 155–185.